WAKE UP

The Morning Routine That Will
Change Your Life

by
Jeff Finley

To all those with the courage to live life on their own terms, in alignment with their truth and their hearts. Because of you, I know it's possible. Thank you.

What's Inside?

Acknowledgements

Thank you to everyone who helped me write this book. Thanks to Hal Elrod for inspiring me to wake up early and Tony Stubblebine and Esther Crawford at Coach.me for encouraging me to teach the habit. Thanks to my editors and proofreaders Kathy Kovacic, Kim Finley, Shellah Inman, Rob Filardo, and Natasha Lynn. And finally, thank you, the reader, for taking time to read my story. I hope this book inspires you in some way.

INTRODUCTION

I'm writing these words at 5:51 a.m., which is earlier than I typically wake up. I couldn't get back to sleep so I decided to stay up and write my book's first page. This is what can happen when you wake up early, before everyone else, to focus on your own personal development.

PERSONAL DEVELOPMENT?

Personal development is kind of a dry term. It doesn't sound very cool or fun. In my opinion, our entire lives should be focused on personal development. It means creating the life we desire and becoming our truest, most authentic self. Then finding the bravery to show it to the world.

I got into personal development when I tried habit-change as a way out of my depression. I used an app on my phone that made it fun to check off habits like push-ups and journaling. Dozens of habits and thousands of check-ins later, I feel safe, not to mention thrilled, to say I'm no longer depressed and happier than ever. This stuff changed my life, seriously. I am writing this book to show you how I did it.

WHY THIS BOOK?

The main reason I wrote this book is because I had to take what I've learned and put it out there. If someone else can benefit, even just a little, that makes me happy.

Some of this stuff is not always easy to talk about with people because not everyone is ready to change their life. I like to think I'm having a conversation with someone else who cares about taking responsibility for their own life as much as I do. It keeps me company. I like that.

WAKE UP

This book is about how to wake up early. But it's more than that. It's about how to wake up to your true self and know your purpose. But first I will show you how you can build the habit of waking up early. Then I'll teach you about the habits that changed my life and how you can implement them into your morning routine.

I'll share what I know about each habit from my own experience and research. I wouldn't say that I'm an expert on these, and I am certainly not a scholar. I'm just a guy who was tired of feeling stuck and hopeless and decided to do something about it.

This book is a little different. Sure it will teach you how you can beat procrastination and learn some new habits. But it's also very personal. I include a lot of my own first-hand experience. Some books like to include studies, statistics, or other factoids to convince you of their points. But to me, those books lack personality. I want you to get to know the person behind the words.

You'll get to know me throughout this book. I hope I can relate some of my struggles and triumphs in a way that inspires you. Because we are all in this together.

I'm not even a "morning person." I would actually consider myself a "night owl" who developed a waking early habit to add more peace and happiness to my life. Not only did it work, but it opened my eyes to a part of myself that I had been ignoring. This I might call my true self.

There are books out there that will teach you how to master habits, get super fit, or meditate like a monk. I've read some of those books and they are amazing. I'm going to give you a splash of what I've learned.

Use this book as a guide to build yourself your own killer morning routine. One that brings you peace, joy, clarity, and purpose. I'll be here rooting you on and if you ever have any questions, you can always email me at jeff82finley@gmail.com

CHAPTER ONE

WAKING UP

We are sleepwalking through life and we don't even know it. Days, weeks, and years pass by and we feel like we haven't been able to catch our breath. We work hard at being a good person, employee, or spouse but end up overworked, distracted, stressed out, and depressed. It's confusing because we are sold happiness in a coffee mug, beer bottle, new clothes, fast food, and entertainment. We know it's empty. But how do we wake up to real happiness?

ഇരു

My Story

Let me start by telling you my story. When I started tracking my habits in 2012, I was pretty deep into depression. This was just one thing that helped bring hope and inspiration back into my life. I had been battling burnout in my work life and stagnation everywhere else. For seven or eight years, I had been putting much of myself into my career as a graphic designer and business owner.

I loved almost every minute of it, but the last two to three years I started to feel tired and no longer motivated by the fame and fortune that inspired me before. I used to care about being a big deal, but I was tired.

This lack of motivation was mysterious. I'd always been somewhat of an attention seeker, but in a positive way. As a childhood artist growing up, I got a lot of attention for my drawings. I even had a friend in middle school who collected my work and I felt important.

WAKE UP

After art school, I was offered a partnership at the design firm Go Media in 2006. They were impressed with how I had made a name for myself as a freelance designer for the music industry at a young age. They liked how I got excited about social media and online marketing. I thought of us like a band of rock stars (except we were designers) and wanted to take the world by storm!

We built up quite a following and even had some incredible years financially. I am really proud of the work that we produced together and the opportunities that arose as a result. I was able to design t-shirts and posters for a living and then even write a book about it called *Thread's Not Dead*. We started selling leftover illustrations as stock images and it turned into half of our company business! In the midst of all this, I started a conference for creators called Weapons of Mass Creation (WMC Fest) and that became my big focus the past couple of years.

When I look back on it, I felt like I was living and working my dream. But as the years passed

I found myself getting more burned out. I didn't care about getting famous anymore. We had our moments, but it became a grind trying to recreate the magic over and over. We were endlessly searching for that "next big thing" and I felt like I exhausted all my great ideas and had nothing left in the tank.

The conference I was running turned into a full-time job as an organizer, and I was leaving behind the creative work that I had been doing all my life as an artist. I missed it.

The burnout led to feelings of guilt because I wasn't *supposed* to feel this way. From the outside looking in, I *was* living the dream! I had a ton of creative freedom and autonomy, a good income, and had respect and adoration from my peers. What more could I want?

That guilt led to depression and for a good year, year-and-a-half, I was miserable. I think I was hurting projects more than I helped. I mustered up courage to come to work every day and I always saw the glass half empty. I no longer was my optimistic, positive self. This went on and it wasn't until January 2013 that I told my business partners I was depressed.

Boy was that scary. I avoided telling them for so long. I felt ashamed for being depressed and holding back the company. I felt guilty for asking for help, too. I didn't even know what I wanted, I just knew I wasn't interested.

I laced up my boots and toughed it out like any responsible person would. I co-organized another successful year of WMC Fest and we saw attendance rise and more national eyeballs were taking notice. However, my contribution to the organization was becoming less as my event director and core team started doing the majority of the heavy lifting.

Organizing the event became a huge burden on me year after year and I just wanted out. I felt guilty for wanting to quit something that was gaining momentum and was looked at as an inspiring event that made the world a better place. What kind of person bails on that?

At some point, I started finding relief in articles in Leo Babauta's *Zen Habits*. Articles that turned my attention toward a simpler life. A life focused more on the present moment and enjoying the simple things. This seemed *extraordinary* to me. I got excited about an article I read about having no goals anymore. That tells you where I was!

Reading articles on *Zen Habits* inspired me in many different ways. One, I loved the calmness and clarity. And two, I loved the idea of building positive habits.

I tried a few, like decluttering or single tasking, but never was able to stick with any. I tried meditating, but I didn't get any more out of it other than a brief moment of escape before I had to enter the real world again. I tried taking one of Leo's clutter-free courses but wasn't able to stick to the habit of getting rid of things daily.

The *idea* of positive habits stuck, though. Changing enough small things about my day that it could lead to a more profound lifestyle change in the end was enough to get me back on my path.

I started reading more about habits and found people like James Clear and Nathan Barry. I downloaded the *Headspace* app to learn more about meditation. Around this time is when *Lift* came out and I felt inspired by the beautiful design and the ability to create a list of daily habits on my phone and check them off each day. It kept track and the community gave me positive encouragement for keeping streaks alive.

I started adding habits to improve my diet, health, and well-being. This was all good, except I could not consistently do it. I would settle back into old habits and routines and I would become apathetic toward keeping the habits up. I knew when I was doing these I was happier and felt productive. But when I wasn't, I felt sad and depressed.

If I could only find the time.

I felt like if I could carve out time every day to do my habits, I'd have more success. I decided the solution was to *start waking up early*. I hated the idea at first, but it was pretty much the only way I knew I could do it. In a moment of inspiration I set my alarm for one hour earlier. The very first day I missed my alarm and woke up late! The first week was very rocky and I quickly gave up.

Around this time I read the book the *Power of Habit* - which taught me about triggers, routines, and rewards. This was something I actually remembered from *Zen Habits* but never put into practice. If I could make getting up early a habit, I knew I'd fill it with the positive habits that made me happier.

I needed a good reward for getting up early. So I started by watching an addictive TV series every day. I just had to crawl over to the couch and turn on Netflix and I'd consider that a win. I would sip my coffee and the show would hold my attention long enough for me to wake up. After it was over, I had about 30 minutes before I needed to get ready for work, so I did my push-ups, reading, and a few other habits.

That worked out pretty well, but I started to slip as I got bored easily and wasn't getting much sleep. I wasn't going to bed any earlier so that made it hard.

Right around then was when I found the book *The Miracle Morning* by Hal Elrod. It was highly rated on Amazon and I decided to pick it up. Boy this was a *game changer* and just what I needed! In fact, I highly recommend you read it as well!

Hal's book made me look at my morning routine in a completely different light. It blew the doors wide open. In fact, this was the first time I had ever heard the words "personal development." Actually, that's not true. I remember coming across Steve Pavlina's blog *Personal Development for Smart People* several years prior, but it didn't appeal to me at the time. Hal was the first one who made it sink in. He quoted one of his favorite people Jim Rohn, "Your level of success will seldom exceed your level of personal development."

It was this focus on personal development that excited me. It was a complete lifestyle change. A paradigm shift. For most of my life I felt like I needed to focus on things *outside* of myself to become successful. I thought I needed to build things in this world that earned me money and respect which would translate into success and happiness. I thought I was only as good as the work I produced. And if nobody cared about it, then nobody cared about me.

I realized I was wrong. It works the other way around. I needed to care about *me*.

The idea of "achieving happiness" never really entered my life until I started to feel depressed the majority of the time. I wondered what happened to my happiness. Where did it go? I had it most of my life, but suddenly it was missing?

Personal development and happiness became my new mission.

Personal development is about working on becoming the best version of yourself. Everything in your life is an opportunity for growth and learning. It's about letting go of limiting beliefs that hold you back and embracing ones that bring you truth, love, and empowerment. Steve Pavlina uses the phrase "live consciously" which is essentially a reminder to stop sleepwalking through life. Wake up to the present moment and live it thoroughly.

Put another way, live *on purpose*. Consciously *choose* what you do while having full awareness of this choice. You shift your perspective from "reality happens to me" to "I create my reality." And that is a powerful paradigm shift.

Most people live a state of consciousness that one might consider unconscious. There is a certain level of self-awareness we have at different times in our lives. We spend our days reacting and putting out fires and answering to other people.

Every day becomes filled with other people's priorities and we often find ourselves with hardly any time to ourselves.

This is why people use the biggest excuse of all, "I don't have enough time" to do things they know are good for them. They prioritize everyone else in their life. This is noble, but it's misguided. People come and go, but there is one person who you spend your entire life with, and that's *you!* How much time do you spend doing things that make you happy? Do you do those things on purpose? Do you know if those things are actually bringing you happiness? Or a temporary escape?

I challenge you to look at your life differently.

Look at it through the lens of the ultimate creator. What kind of life would you design for yourself? What's the most fulfilling and rewarding life you could experience?

In my opinion, life is to be enjoyed, not endured. If you can shift your perspective to one that *you* are the creator of your life, rather than simply a victim of circumstances, you start to feel the power. You are responsible for the good *and the bad* in your life. Once you realize that, your whole world can open up. If you give yourself permission to dream and fantasize about what you can create for yourself in this life, knowing it can actually come true: life gets a whole lot more exciting!

Let's get this started, shall we?

We're going to carve out time to work, play, and *be* with ourselves every day. We do that by waking up early before everyone else. That time is our precious <u>me</u> time. There's a reason Hal Elrod called it the *Miracle Morning*. It's not about getting up early to check email or get more done in the day. You will find it to be quite the contrary!

Doing less is oftentimes more fulfilling when done consciously. You can look at waking early as a productivity habit, but try to think of it as the most sacred time of your day. The one that only *you* understand and truly know. The time where you get to be honest, authentic, and truly heard. That's because you are allowing yourself time to be with and care for yourself like nobody ever has.

What Does it Mean to Wake Up?

We all wake up in the morning after a night's sleep, right? So by definition, the act of waking up implies that we had previously been asleep. While this book is most definitely about waking up early, it's also about waking up another way. Waking up to your true self. Your true purpose.

Waking up to your true self implies a different level of awakening. A profound realization. Some might call it enlightenment, but that's another topic. Like I said before, many people look like they are awake in this world, running around, driving from place to place, typing on their keyboards and smartphones, or chatting with friends and family.

But the truth is they are in fact asleep. They are dreaming. They are just unaware of the dream.

WAKE UP

Author Don Miguel Ruiz talks about humanity's collective dream of the planet. We live in a reactive world of multi-tasking and distraction. The idea of there being a different way of living, a simpler one that brings more joy and authenticity seems too far out.

The idea that a life of enjoyment and fulfillment instead of suffering and stress seems like the dream we all wish we were dreaming instead.

The encouraging thing is more and more people *are* waking up. There are Facebook groups and Reddit communities, for example. Just do a quick Google search on humanity's shift to higher consciousness. We are also waking up to our spiritual essences without the need for religion or dogma. Even our supernormal and extrasensory abilities like intuition and "the clairs" are coming online! These are needed in a world that is becoming increasingly dependent on left-brain logic, technology, and artificial intelligence. And don't get me started on *Starseed* activations!

It's really an exciting time to be alive!

The good news is that it's 100% attainable by everyone right now. To say that it's far off is like saying that it's a destination or somewhere to get to. But in reality, it's merely a mindset switch. A lightbulb going off. An "aha" moment.

An awakening.

Take four minutes and listen to Alan Watts's The Dream of Life on YouTube and see what I mean.

Have you ever visualized the life of your dreams? Have you ever actually given it more than a passing thought? Like I said, for most of us, the life of our dreams doesn't seem attainable. We're conditioned to believe we have to be a certain way, to have a certain job. We are conditioned to work hard and sacrifice and wait for it to pay off in the future.

I don't know about you, but I don't want to wait for the future. I want to live the life of my dreams right now. I want the same for you.

There are many books out there about pursuing your passion, quitting your job, starting your own business, etc. The idea of pursuing your dreams is definitely not uncommon. But in a world where so many people are encouraged to pursue their dreams, why are so many of us scared, worried, and depressed?

I will be the first to tell you that the whole idea is extremely difficult. Because for most of my life, I thought I was doing just that! I knew from an early age I wanted to be an artist of some type. So I lined up my college education and career choices around it. And I definitely had success and even had a taste of fame here and there. I had some exciting years, but after awhile I found myself unhappy and eventually depressed.

WHAT IS DEPRESSION?

I'm not going to give you a clinical version of depression. It's not a disorder or disease or something you catch. It's not something you cure with drugs. To me, depression is a *stifled soul*. And to cure it, we must look at what our soul needs. Generally it's some form of creative expression that is yearning to come out. And for whatever reason, we don't let it. Are we too afraid of being who we really are?

The soul speaks to us through intuition and emotions such as inspiration and joy. We all know what those feel like. But if you are consistently unable to act on your inspirations, then the body begins to shut down. Our minds develop defense mechanisms to keep us safe and we feel that if we acted on our inspirations, we might disrupt the security of the life we have created for ourselves.

As children we loved to express ourselves creatively. It comes naturally. But as we grow up, we are domesticated. We are taught what it means to be an adult and how to get a job and fit into the culture around us. We dial down our expressiveness bit-by-bit. Sometimes we take a job that we don't really want but it pays well. Many aspiring artists, dancers, or writers become engineers, doctors, and lawyers because of well-meaning encouragement from their families and teachers. Not to say those fields are bad, but we are raised to fit into a certain role in life.

Fitting into that role is often rewarded very well. Getting good grades in school, behaving properly, pleasing the right people to get ahead... Those are all rewarded with praise, money, and advancement. We feel good about those things and we feel like we're making progress. As the years go by, we start to grow tired. It starts to feel like a rat race. If we are lucky, our childhood passions might have become hobbies or pastimes, but many of us are too busy working and pleasing other people that we have no time for ourselves.

To battle the fatigue and burnout, we consume caffeine and prescription drugs to make us feel alert and focused. Instead of being told how to cultivate our own energy levels, we are sold energy in a can or coffee mug. And instead of being educated on how to relieve stress naturally, many rely on alcohol and television to relax or escape from their problems. An ever-increasing sense of discontent and unease grows within us. We feel stuck. We've come this far, we don't want quit. We don't want to lose what we have. It seems our culture has developed a genius system of keeping us perpetually tired and discontent so it can sell us products that temporarily relieve the symptoms, but don't cure the problem.

We are conditioned into this lifestyle from an early age. The idea of "you can be anyone you want to be" is something we are all taught. But you can only pick from a few choices! What about being who you really are?

I believe I was lucky. My parents and peers picked up on my creative abilities when I was young and encouraged me all the way. My Dad never liked his jobs and didn't like authority much either. My Mom was about as supportive as you can imagine, and helped me believe that I could actually achieve what I set my mind to. They didn't try to tell me to be anyone other than who I wanted. They didn't want "the man" getting me down. I gravitated toward alternative culture, punk rock, and DIY folk music and had an affinity for their raw, independent lifestyle, minus the drugs and alcohol.

Despite being encouraged to be myself, I still adapted to try to fit in and make a living. At the time I wasn't even aware of it. There's a blend of knowing what I want to do and knowing what my options are. And then trying to fit them together. It always seemed like there was a gatekeeper or some other authority figure in the way of letting me "in." I would come across resistance like this all the time. Out of desperation, fear, or necessity I would do things that I thought I should do. Like spend tens of thousands of dollars on a college education. If I knew then what I know now, I might have reconsidered.

When I admitted I was depressed in 2013, it was something I never thought I'd say. I had always believed I was living a great life that had purpose and clarity, but it started to get foggy after awhile. I said "yes" to many things I probably should have said "no" to. I let people into my life that dug at my self esteem and distracted my attention away from my passions. I was trying to please so many people and felt like I was spread way too thin. This created a fractured soul. There were many times I wanted to just throw it all away.

I had to look my depression squarely in the eye. I had to look at my habits and tendencies. I had to consciously make time to focus on my own well being. So that's why I started getting up early in the first place. To create time for me. It wasn't selfish, it was necessary. I envisioned a morning that was peaceful and calm without distractions. I pictured myself doing yoga, meditating, and sipping tea as I watched the sun rise. That seemed so much more real and authentic than trying to figure out why our social media posts don't have as many "likes" as they used to. Sigh.

So in June of 2013, my morning routine was born. I had no idea that it would change my life completely.

CHAPTER TWO

HOW TO BUILD HABITS

In order to make time to build a life changing morning routine, we need to build the habit of waking up early. This will give us a foundation to where all other habits will fit. From my own personal experience, the wake-up-early habit was indeed the most life changing habit I've ever done. Simply because it carved out the space for me to consistently do all these other great habits.

ജ

Mistakes and Excuses

Before we dive in, let's get the excuses out of the way. Most people who try to wake up early encounter the same problems. Here's a list of the most common ones. I will get into solutions for these problems later in the book.

Not enough time. This is the biggest excuse in the book. We all have 24 hours in a day. And we all have free will to make choices on how we spend those 24 hours. Can you do it?

Not enough willpower. This is another common complaint. Here's the thing, willpower is like a muscle. And sometimes our muscles are weak if we don't use them a lot. If we aren't used to exercising, we tire easily. Willpower is just like that. If we rely on willpower alone, we're going to burn out fast. In the *Overcoming Challenges* chapter, I will teach you ways to conserve and strengthen your willpower and make it easy.

I need more sleep. When people start waking

up early, they usually sacrifice sleep to make the time. This is actually OK at first, but it catches up with them later. There are many factors that go into feeling rested and excited for your morning routine no matter how many hours of sleep you get. I will show you some strategies and tips that will put this excuse to rest!

I can't stay motivated. Welcome to the club. I'm writing this book and sometimes I can't stay motivated. It's something all of us face. I have been burnt out and have killed my morning routine before. But I somehow find a way to get back on and get inspired.

I keep hitting snooze. I used to hit the snooze several times every morning before I would get up. I'd set my alarm a half hour earlier just so I could hit snooze a few times! But I figured out a way to never hit snooze again, and it's simpler than you think.

My brain is foggy in the morning. Well of course it is, you just woke up! We can't expect to be alert and ready to go as soon as we wake up. This groggy state is usually so uncomfortable that all we can think about is going back to bed. It clouds our view of our routines and habits. Everything looks grey and dull. It's hard to be excited when you're looking through the fog. But I've got a fresh perspective that I think could make this experience more pleasant.

I have kids or family obligations. I will admit that I cannot truly know what it's like to have kids and be responsible for other people in that way. But what I do know is that many successful people with children found that waking up early before the kids was entirely possible. They just had to adjust their schedule and priorities.

I'm burnt out. When I first started my morning routine, I was so excited I couldn't even sleep the night before. After awhile I started to get bored and lose interest. I wasn't getting enough sleep and the excitement wore off. I'll get into how to deal with burnout or the urge to quit in the *Overcoming Challenges* chapter later in this book.

I'm bored. This is similar to being burnt out. The excitement of your routine will inevitably wear thin and you will get bored. This is a fact. But again, we are in control of our routine. We have free will and can make choices on what to do about it. Sometimes we get in a groove, and that feels good. But then it turns into a rut and we are stuck. I'll show you how to keep your mornings fresh.

Change Your Habits, Change Your Life

Have you thought about habit change before? Have you ever considered what you do every day? A lot of people run their lives on autopilot and in their words, "it's all a blur." One day bleeds into the next and they are too deep into reacting and catching up that they cannot take a step back.

Before I got into habit-change, I was still somewhat of a self-help nerd. I loved reading blog articles on 10 Ways to Be More Productive, or 15 Hacks to Better Email Management. I did read books on lifestyle design such as Tim Ferriss' *The*

4 *Hour Workweek*. I always seemed to look at life as a constant learning process. I enjoyed trying new apps and tools that could give me some sort of edge in saving time, being more productive, or even as far as making me happier.

But over time all these productivity hacks and efficiency boosters seemed to get on my nerves. I was addicted to productivity porn. You know, where you spend more time reading about productivity than actually being productive? Where it's more fun to try out yet another to-do list app instead of just getting stuff done?

I became a big fan of GTD, the *Getting Things Done* methodology. I loved the idea of "Inbox Zero." I loved the idea of treating my life like an ongoing project. But if anyone's ever tried GTD, it's hard to maintain. We eventually fall back into old habits. I did many times. I started to become overwhelmed and even productivity porn wasn't interesting to me anymore. Coincidentally, this was near the time I was falling into depression.

WAKE UP

While reading *Zen Habits* in the late 2000s, Leo Babauta's perspectives on habit change really resonated with me. I would credit him for being the spark that caused me to look at my habits with the intention of changing them.

Most of what we do every day is habitual. From the time we wake up in the morning, we have habits. Brushing our teeth, showering, making coffee or breakfast, driving the same route to work every day. At work we have habits, like checking email first thing in the morning. We are checking our phones or social media every time we are waiting for something. We tend to get lunch the same time and same way every day. We eat the same kinds of things for dinner. We pretty much have a routine that we have settled into whether we like it or not.

When I started looking at my own routines, most of it was built around other people's obligations and requests of me. Is yours like that? Think about it. My wake up time was dictated by having to be at the office at a certain time. At work, there was always a barrage of email requests, inter-office chats, meetings, and client projects. After work was the same routine of making dinner, taking a nap, doing chores, watching TV if I had time, spending time online, etc. I did make sure to have time for hobbies like making music, breakdancing, or reading. But largely, my routine was pretty routine if you know what I mean.

During my depression, this stuff started to get to me. I started to feel overwhelmed. Even my self-initiated projects were taking on a life of their own and I found myself doing things I didn't really want to do. But in the background, I kept finding inspiration from *Zen Habits*. The idea of a simpler life kept nagging at me. But what was I doing about it?

Leo wrote a post on *Zen Habits* about becoming an early-riser and creating a morning ritual. This idea seemed lovely to me. But like so many of us these days, the only action I took was a Tweet and a Facebook share. I must not have been that committed. But over time, this idea of becoming an early riser kept coming back. Leo's approach to a simpler life and being deliberate about everything you do made me happy. I was ready for a change, I just didn't know when it was going to happen.

When I found the habit-change app *Coach.me* (it was called Lift at the time), I could enter in any habit I wanted and check into daily. It would track my streaks and give me encouragement. A cool feature was that other users could give me "props" for completing habits and I could do the same for them. Some of the more popular habits like meditation would have thousands of people doing it. And if I didn't know what habits to do, I could simply browse through the app and try new ones. If I didn't like it, I could dump it.

Suddenly habit-change was fun. Here was my motivation to get started. The app used popular gamification principles and a clean reward system to encourage you to check in daily. I started adding all sorts of habits. Meditation was a big one as it was a perfect escape from my stressful days. I would also take on habits like drink more water, exercise, walk, yoga, stretch, gratitude, etc.

My experience using the app taught me a lot about habits. I started noticing which habits I checked into frequently and which ones I put off until tomorrow. I started noticing what habits felt difficult and which ones were easy. And I started noticing how good I would feel checking off habits on a daily basis. I felt like I was getting somewhere.

Unlike a video game, I wasn't making progress in some virtual world. I was making progress on things that were important to me. It got me thinking a lot more about what was *actually* important to me. Knowing I could turn any goal or aspiration into a habit allowed me to reflect on my life and start choosing my actions more consciously.

Another thing happened when I started checking into these habits. I wanted to learn more about them. What was meditation exactly? I knew it as a stress reliever and that's about it. It's like when you pick up a guitar and start playing for the first time, it doesn't sound good at all. At first it's fun to make noise, but after awhile you want to know how to make music. And so I would read up on meditation or eating better. I would read about habit change in general. The book *The Power of Habit* was huge.

The Power of Habit is one of the best books about habits. It taught me a few lessons. One important lesson is the cue, routine, reward pattern. But instead of cue, I like to use the word trigger.

The 3 Keys to Habit Change

The three keys are trigger, routine, and reward. Trigger is how a habit starts. It's the thing that sets you off. For example, let's say your habit is brushing your teeth. Your trigger is simply waking up in the morning. Or every time you have to wait for something, you look at your phone or open a new tab.

Routine is the activity that takes place after you are triggered. This includes doing the habit. So after waking up, your routine is going to the bathroom and brushing your teeth. And after that brief moment of boredom, your routine is to get your phone out and scroll through Twitter, Facebook, email, Instagram, Reddit, or whatever distraction you enjoy.

The reward is that pleasurable feeling that reinforces the habit. It's what keeps us coming back for more. When you brush your teeth, you have that clean-mouth feeling afterward. When you look at your phone, you're looking for that little rush of positive emotion from a new message, comment, or email. Or the novelty of new information.

Leo also talked about this pattern. Since our habits are built on this pattern, how can you use this to create *good* habits for yourself?

It's easier to start looking at our current habits and becoming mindful of our triggers. Take one of your worst habits, one you'd love to change. It could be smoking, drinking alcohol, eating sweets, or playing video games too long. Then look at what triggers those habits.

In my podcast episode on habits, my co-host George, a former smoker, explained that his triggers were often social in nature. If someone else was smoking, he was more likely to smoke. If he felt anxious around people, he might escape outside to light one up and get a break from the action. If he was feeling stressed, he might reach for a cigarette.

This was a great discovery! Because once you are able to recognize your triggers, you are more likely to be able to change your habit.

We know that smoking is notoriously hard to quit because nicotine is an addictive substance. And most of the "rewards" we get from our habits are the result of some sort of addiction. Usually it's because of the release of "feel good" chemicals in our brain like dopamine, serotonin, or endorphins.

Now that you have thought about what triggers

your habits, what is the routine? For coffee lovers, there's perhaps a morning ritual surrounding their coffee making. For yoga or meditation, maybe you light some incense and say a quiet prayer or mantra before you start. It's the cycle of actions you take surrounding your habit.

For me, whenever I'd sit down to watch TV, I would feel the temptation to grab a snack first. My snack of choice was a bowl of cereal. I'd be triggered by turning on the TV, then I'd go through my routine of pouring myself a bowl of cereal and plopping down on the couch and hitting "play" on whatever it was I was watching.

And what are the rewards for performing your habit? What are you actually getting out of it? Is it a relief of stress or tension? Is it a soothing feeling of comfort? Is it the feeling of being liked, accepted, or involved? Is it the satisfaction of being in-the-know? Identifying your rewards is important because it helps you learn about what your cravings, likes, needs, and desires are. We can later use those rewards to help us build positive new habits. Now that you've thought about the trigger, routine, and reward pattern for some of your habits, let's try to create a new one. What's it going to be? Well, the most obvious one for this book is the wake-up-early habit. Not just because it's the subject of this book, but because it's a keystone habit.

Habit	Trigger	Routine	Reward
brushing your teeth	morning alarm sounds	go to bathroom, brush your teeth	clean-mouth feeling, more awake
checking your phone	brief moment of boredom, waiting	check social media with no real purpose	avoided boredom, feeling of being caught up
snacking during TV	TV turns on	get a snack, press play	tasty snack, watch TV
smoking	socially anxious	go outside to smoke	avoided uncomfortable situation
make the bed	wake up, step out of bed	make the bed look tidy	feeling of accomplishment

Keystone Habits

A keystone habit is one that inspires other positive habits around it. For example, if you exercise, you are more likely to eat healthy, and drink more water. One great example of a keystone habit is the simple act of making the bed in the morning. Making the bed is a really easy habit to do.

The trigger is waking up and stepping out of bed. The routine is to simply organize the blankets and pillows in a way that looks nice to you. The reward is seeing a tidy bed and the satisfaction of accomplishing something as soon as you start the day.

When done deliberately like this, it sets a tone of positive progress in your life. As little as it is, what this habit does is help rewire your brain to be more effective at accomplishing things. This easy success helps you get inspired to add other habits to your life. It helps turn you into a person that consciously changes their lifestyle and habits. It's so simple, yet so profound.

WAKE UP

The wake-up-early habit is not just a keystone habit, it's a *breakthrough* habit. One that breaks through the well-defined routines and ruts you are in and exposes new, fresh territory to be explored. It creates a gap of time in your daily schedule that you can fill with positive habits as you choose.

Waking up early doesn't require special skills either. It's simply an exercise in self-discipline and self-care. If you wake up early, you are more likely to do the things that move your life in the direction you desire.

Before I started waking up early, I was inconsistent with my habits. I would try to find time in my normal routine to do them and sometimes I would completely forget. I was overwhelmed already and trying to find time to meditate and exercise in my already busy routine was harder than I thought.

To make it easier, *Zen Habits* recommends only doing one habit at a time. I like that idea because our mental energy is focused on a lot less. We can make one habit happen, right? I suggest doing one at a time until you feel ready to add more. So the one habit we will focus on first is building the breakthrough keystone habit of waking up early.

Wake Up Early With Ease

The simplest way to start waking up early is to set your alarm earlier and then do it.

It's as simple as that, really. But why is that so hard? Most of us feel like time is scarce and sleep is precious. So the idea of sacrificing sleep feels like the worst idea of all time. Waking up before you *have* to? Forget about it!

By now you should be inspired enough to want to make a change in your life. Most people aren't. You're reading this book so you must have some motivation already. Let's put it to use!

We have to turn waking up early into a habit? Why? Because habits reduce the need for willpower.

When your alarm is going off and it's dark and cold in your bedroom, your willpower is extremely low. We are usually warm, comfortable, and half asleep and the easiest thing to do is to go back to sleep. Even when we decided that getting up early was good for us.

We want to use as little willpower as possible because habits allow us to work on autopilot. We don't need willpower to brush our teeth or take a shower—at least not all the time! We don't need willpower to drive to work, because it's so ingrained in our routine. We need willpower to start something, but to keep it going we need to build it into a habit. The easiest way to start the wake up early routine is to make it fun.

Mornings Should be Fun

Try to remember a time when waking up early felt effortless. A time when you couldn't resist getting out of bed. You jumped out of bed. You woke up even earlier because you were so excited! You could hardly sleep the night before!

You've got to have some mornings like that in your life, right? For many of us, Christmas morning as a child was one of those mornings. As children, that morning was filled with magic, curiosity, wonder, and of course, loads of presents under the tree! The anticipation was killing us. So we sprang out of bed. There were mornings where my siblings and I tore open presents before my parents even got up. I feel bad for them now!

Other times I remember being excited to wake up were mornings when we would be going on vacation or on a trip of some kind. Maybe something special was happening at school and I just couldn't wait to go. Maybe someone made you breakfast in bed?

When was the last time you were that excited to wake up in the morning?

What was it about Christmas and those special occasions that made it so compelling to wake up early? It didn't even matter how much sleep we got the night before. And often we could hardly sleep because we were so excited.

How can we instill even just a fraction of that level of excitement into our mornings? What would surely motivate us to get up early?

For me, I know this is hardly "Christmas-like" but I used my mild addiction to watching TV shows like Breaking Bad and The Wire to my advantage. Instead of watching it at night, I watched in the morning. I set my alarm 90 minutes earlier and was actually excited to wake up and watch the show. I'd be eating breakfast and drinking coffee. And this really worked for me in the beginning because it got me out of bed. That, and the thrill of doing something new and bold like waking up before the sun came up!

By the time the show was over, I was awake. I still had some time before I had to start getting ready for work so I used that time to work on my other habits like meditation and reading. My morning was already so much better than before! I checked off "wake up early" off my habit list, as well as several others. All this happened before I left for work and I was already more productive. I started feeling great about my ability to accomplish things. I was making time for myself.

Just a Little Every Day

Finally, the last bit of advice on habit change is this. Keep it small. Keep it tiny. Habit expert BJ Fogg writes a lot about this and it's one of the core fundamentals that *Coach.me* was based on. It's all about bite-sized chunks that you can do every day without a lot of willpower.

Lets break down exercise as an example. My previous stints with exercise went like this: I'd go long periods without exercise and suddenly have a realization that I was getting fat, lazy, and out of shape. So I would feel bad about myself and then go to the gym or hire a personal trainer and work out really hard. I'd go for a long jog around the neighborhood. I would have a couple of days or weeks of accomplishment, but eventually would grow tired keeping up with this. I even signed up for a gym membership under a two-year contract at $50/month. I went three times.

Do you see my problem? I did too much. I put too much pressure on myself and set the bar really high. Not only have I observed myself following this pattern, but several of my coaching clients do the same thing. It's in our nature. We get a spark of inspiration and energy and we use all of it at once and we burn out. We are unable to maintain our intensity over the long term.

The secret is just doing a little bit every day. Over time this adds up to huge change.

Jeff Olson wrote an entire book about this called *The Slight Edge*. It's another one of those game-changer books that I really recommend. Whether you call it tiny habits, the slight edge, or baby steps, it's all the same. Start small and set the bar really low.

Instead of the on-again, off-again habit of exercise, I wanted to build a sustainable habit that kept me moving every day. I told my life coach Dr. Jody Stanislaw that I wanted to exercise three days a week. And she told me to do even less! She said go to the gym once a week. "Put it on your calendar," she said. "If you schedule it, it will get done."

If you only commit to once a week, you take the pressure off yourself all those other days. I found when the time came for me to go to the gym, I was really excited for it. And relieved I didn't have to go any other day that week.

Then I started feeling a desire to want to go again. And this is when you should raise the bar, when you feel a genuine desire. Not when you feel like you *should*. I have learned that "shoulds" are not the proper motivator for human beings with a soul. True desire is. I read a great article called The Crossroads of Should vs. Must. Look it up.

My point is, Jody recommended starting really small and building slowly. This creates lasting change. She has seen it time and time again with her clients. I really recommend this method too.

WAKE UP

But let me provide a counterpoint.

Sometimes we just need to start off with a BANG! Why do so many people sign up for marathons? Or want to climb Mt. Everest? You don't see people out there hiking over the hill in their neighborhood hoping one day they'll eventually make it to Everest? Sometimes setting a big goal can spark an immense amount of inspiration and creativity.

We will need to combine the BANG with the baby steps. You need to create a bang to clear the space and then use baby steps to fill the space and sustain it.

I've seen people try to start waking up early with small increments like five minutes, then ten minutes, etc. I don't think it works very well because what do you honestly think having five extra minutes is going to do for you? What's the motivation? It's gone in a snap! Waking up five minutes early is like not waking up early at all. You aren't actually creating much space.

I recommend one hour early to start. Or if that scares you, try doing only 30 minutes. But if 60 scares you, I think you should try it. It's not like running a marathon. You don't need any extra skill to wake up 60 minutes early as opposed to five.

Remember, it's about *blowing shit up* and creating a space of your own. That's what this is all about. And in this case it's go big or go home.

The tiny habits will apply to the individual habits that make up our morning routine. When I started, I woke up 90 minutes early because the shows I was watching were almost an hour long. It was a necessity! But if you don't plan on using this technique, then 30 minutes should be fine.

After you get up 30-60 minutes early at first, you'll discover you want even more time. You'll crave getting up even earlier! That's how we can build on this habit.

The baby step approach could apply to waking up early but only doing this routine a few days a week. The problem with that is it's hard to build consistency with your sleep schedule. If you aren't ready to go all the way, then maybe do it once a week and see what it's like. Or do it on workdays, and sleep in on weekends. But most sleep experts say you should consistently wake up at the same time every day to build your rhythm. If you sleep in every other day, it's hard to get into a nice rhythm.

Having said all this, there is no right or wrong way. The whole point is to notice your tendencies and where you get stuck. Try waking up early for a week or two and see how it goes. What went wrong and what went right? How can you improve it? Did you give yourself enough time?

Once the initial excitement subsides, you'll need to rely on another critical point: *knowing what you're going to do* the next morning. For now, let's take it one step at a time. Build the wake up early habit until you are ready to start adding stuff to it. The first step is to blow a hole in your routine.

CHAPTER THREE

CREATE YOUR IDEAL MORNING ROUTINE

We've had enough backstory and motivation, let's get down to business! The following sections will teach you about the different habits that are known for their life-changing benefits. I use them in my routine and will share my experience.

After you learn about all these amazing habits, you will be able to mix and match them to create a routine that works for you.

ଚ୨୯ଃ

Morning Routine Basics

A typical morning routine looks like this:

Time	Activity	Duration
6:30 a.m.	wake up, bathroom, brush teeth	15 min.
6:45 a.m.	make coffee, eat breakfast	15 min.
7:00 a.m.	meditate	15 min.
7:15 a.m.	affirmations, gratitude	5 min.
7:20 a.m.	journaling	15 min.
7:35 a.m.	exercise, yoga	25 min.
8:00 a.m.	go for walk	20 min.
8:20 a.m.	read book	20 min.
8:40 a.m.	shower	20 min.

See how I broke it down into time blocks? This is a must.

Any good morning routine has a framework like this. You can be flexible of course, but it really helps to write it out. If you are a smart phone user you can use an app like *Seconds*, an interval timer on my iPhone. I used to use A.M. Routine which worked pretty nicely. You can input all your activities and give them a time limit and it will help keep you on schedule. This is helpful in the beginning when you are just getting started.

Half the battle is simply knowing what you are going to do in the morning! Waking up early without knowing what you are going to do is guaranteed to fail. Don't believe me, try it for a few days and see how long you last before you give up and sleep in.

I woke up early and didn't have a plan and it took a ton of willpower to stay up. Having a plan reduces the need for willpower. When you go to bed knowing the first thing you will do in the morning, you are so much more likely to feel alert and awake when you get up.

And when you finally establish your routine as a habit, then you don't even have to think! You just naturally do it. That's where we want to get. Before we get into customizing your routine, let's just talk about the different habits you can do.

Finding Clarity and Inner Peace

The first habit I want to get into is *meditation*. Specifically, mindfulness meditation. It's one of the most important habits we can do to truly get to know ourselves. I have been meditating almost daily for two years as of this writing and have experienced many benefits as a result. You can listen to me talk about this on my podcast at http://makermistaker.com/meditation

WHAT MEDITATION HAS DONE FOR ME

My first meditation started as a stress reliever. An escape from the day-to-day barrage of emails, tweets, meetings, and responsibilities. After awhile, I saw most of my stress was coming from repetitive thoughts and fears. Meditation helped me see my thoughts and emotions as separate from myself and this gave me a profound sense of peace.

Being the witness to your thoughts and emotions is commonly called mindfulness. As mindfulness became a habit, I noticed I would be mindful, or aware, even during times I was not sitting in meditation.

Through this mindfulness, I started to connect with a deeper part of myself. It led to a realization of my *true self*. There existed a part of me that was free of the trappings of modern life. Free of the obligations, judgments, and opinions. The part of me that wore no masks and was authentically me. I could choose to connect to it any time I wanted.

Even deeper still, the mindfulness habit led me to my first out-of-body experience. This blew the doors of my notion of reality. I have since learned how to have these experiences at will (almost), and have had over 60 out-of-body experiences.

But let me take you back to how I started meditating. If you haven't meditated before, you might relate to this.

HOW I STARTED MEDITATION

When I first heard of meditation, it meant nothing to me. I imagined a new-ager sitting cross-legged in a yoga outfit chanting "Ohm." Or a monk hiding out in a cave wearing a hooded robe. None of those felt like me.

When I was feeling stressed at work, I would leave the office and sit in my car alone. To get away from it all. I felt overwhelmed and this was my only respite. I would sit in silence and sometimes I'd end up falling asleep. When I woke up after a brief 15-20 minute escape, I would feel less stressed.

Little did I know that I might have been meditating. But it wasn't until I found a smart phone app called *Headspace* that I began to understand meditation. I would put my headphones on and a calm voice would guide me to watch my thoughts as if they were clouds in the sky, or ripples in a pond. I could sit and watch the clouds go by and notice my thoughts coming and going without the need to react or get pulled into it. What a relief!

For example, I'd think about a project or person that was causing me grief and my mind would constantly play out scenarios, most of them bad. While watching my thoughts, I felt a strong urge to react. But I didn't, I let the thought pop in, I noticed it, then soon it was gone. Most of the time it was replaced by another thought. And then another. I learned that this was called being mindful.

I felt relieved that, for this brief moment, I didn't have to actually <u>do</u> anything about it. I could just watch them come and go. After ten minutes, I felt a little better. Empowered even. After a few days, I started to really enjoy this "escape" into Headspace. The only problem is, the app eventually wanted me to pay to keep using it and I didn't want to. I stopped using it and fell back into old habits.

WHERE OUR ANXIETY AND STRESS COMES FROM

Then in June 2013, I came across a guy named Sean Webb. He was being interviewed on the *Smart Passive Income* podcast about how emotions work. Sean had created a formula that could predict emotions. He clearly explained how anger, anxiety, happiness, worry, fear and any other emotion you could think of could be predicted by his equation. This was fascinating to me.

Without getting into too much detail, Sean was the first person to turn me onto the idea that all our suffering comes from our expectations, attachments, and perceptions. He explained that as we go through life, we attach ourselves to people, things, and ideas and they become part of our identity. For example, if someone were to criticize our favorite sports team or political affiliation, we feel a reactive emotion in response. As if we are being attacked ourselves.

The emotions we feel depend on the level of attachment we have. For example, a Mom loses a cherished piece of jewelry vs. losing her child. Without a doubt she would feel much more grief about losing her child because she was so much more attached. So attached that it was almost like losing part of herself.

This ever-changing sense of self is called the ego. The concept of ego and attachment was a paradigm shift for me. I started seeing everything in my reality differently. Sean asked a very basic question, "who are you?" And my first answer was something close to my Twitter bio. You know, I'm an artist, entrepreneur, here are the companies I am part of, etc.

And when he told me that's not who I really am, I was stunned. I couldn't believe there could be any other answer. If I'm not a product of everything

I've accomplished in my life, than what am I really? Just a body? Everything I've used to distinguish myself from everyone else was just a ruse?

But what about all this talk on personal branding? And how to stand out in the crowd? As an entrepreneur or artist, we try so hard to be different. As a kid who grew up on heavy metal and punk rock, conformity was for the *masses* and I took pride in not being like everyone else.

I loved my weird movies and screamy music. I loved how I didn't smoke, drink, or do drugs like everyone else. I was an artist. I was also a husband, a b-boy, a drummer, an author and business owner. This was my life! These are all things that I felt gave me a sense of identity and purpose. And he was telling me that this was all fake?

He pointed me to a talk given by Richard Rohr called *True Self, False Self* and it was mind blowing for me at the time. Sean went on to talk about how this false sense of self is the source of all human suffering. It's the constant identification with things, even thought-forms, ideas, concepts, emotions, personalities, and habits.

All the stuff we attach to our sense of self comes and goes. It's changeable. Even our bodies are changeable. Cut off my limbs and I'm still conscious. I can gain weight, lose weight, lose my hair, or even change colors. But there exists, and will always exist, the part of ourselves that never changes. The one that sees all the changes. The one that is aware. It's you. It's who you really are.

YOUR TRUE SELF

When you can recognize the difference between your true self and false self, what results is a profound sense of relief. You don't have to build and maintain this identity that you have created for yourself because it's not really you. And what a relief that is!

When I took this insight into my new meditation habit, it brought new meaning to watching my thoughts float by like clouds.

This is when I became acutely aware of my true self behind the clouds.

There existed a part of me that was always there but I never realized it. The observer. The witness. The silent watcher. This silent watcher was the part that notices the thoughts. The one that feels the emotions. And that thoughts and emotions come and go, but the silent watcher remains.

All the thoughts, mental chatter, judgments and opinions could be observed and thus were outside of myself. I could feel tremendous relief knowing that all of this could fade away and I would still exist, until I am dead. Right?

That's a big question. One that is outside the scope of this book. But I have learned first-hand that I'm more than just my body through conscious out-of-body travel. So even without a body, there still exists a part of you that is conscious and aware. It's amazing isn't it?

HOW TO MEDITATE

Let's talk about the meditation habit for you in a practical sense. How are you going to incorporate it into your life?

If you aren't already meditating, you can start by taking just one minute to sit in silence and watch your thoughts. A common practice is to focus on your breath going in and out. I like to count my breaths. Inhale, one. Exhale, two. Inhale, three. Exhale, four. And so on.

Then when thoughts distract you, just notice it. Observe and take notice. Then go back to counting your breaths. Hopefully you weren't distracted so long you forgot where you left off! But if you did, just start over. Don't feel bad for it. See how far you can get.

You will realize that thoughts are constantly coming in your mind. Each one has a certain magnetic pull. Depending on how emotionally charged a thought is, you can physically feel an energetic tug or temptation to get sucked into it. You'll feel an urge to follow that thought with another, and another. They chain together. They build like a snowball.

Each thought form is alive. And it grows as you give it attention and energy. Eventually these thought forms grow so big that they become real. They will cause you act in physical reality so you are now doing something tangible instead of just thinking.

For example, sometimes I have an idea or inspiration that sparks in my head. I won't act on it right away, but I'll notice my mind keeps coming back to it. The more I think about it, the more it takes shape. It starts to become real in my mind. So much that I am inspired to take action and create something in real life.

This is also true for negative thoughts or fears. Say someone cuts you off in traffic and it causes you to feel slighted. Then that person begins to drive really slowly and that feeling you had starts to turn to frustration. Then they brake suddenly and you have to slam on your brakes. You can feel that frustration turn to anger. This might continue as the anger snowballs into rage. Eventually this energy needs to be released, and you might find yourself angrily speeding past the car while giving the driver the finger as you shout obscenities at him.

Or you could stifle your anger and frustration and internalize it. When you internalize the anger, it might snowball into resentment. Which could manifest itself physically in a myriad of ways. You could blow up on a loved one at the slightest trigger, or you could come down with a serious illness.

Either way, our thoughts are powerful tools of creation. It goes both ways.

Meditation and mindfulness helps you detach your sense of identity from your thoughts. This allows you more control over your mind. It lets you feel safe and secure knowing that you exist beyond your thoughts and emotions. You can then consciously use your thoughts as a tool for creation. Which you do anyway, but you just don't realize it. Being mindful is the first step in understanding your true potential as a creator!

WHY DOESN'T EVERYONE MEDITATE?

Common issues people have with meditation is that they start to confront thoughts and emotions that they have suppressed for years. This can be scary. They notice things about themselves they do not like.

I had a friend tell me she doesn't meditate because she is scared of what she would learn about herself. Yes, the longer you meditate, the deeper you will see into your self. Thoughts will come to you from deeper parts of your psyche that you never realized existed.

You might recognize pain that you had internalized as a child that led you to make dozens of adult decisions without you realizing it. These are moments of insight that any meditator would be proud to discover. But this might make someone scared if they are afraid to truly look in the mirror.

FINDING THE TIME TO MEDITATE

Another common problem is finding time to meditate. We all have the same number of hours in the day, but people always make excuses not to take a break. It only takes a couple of minutes to stop the unconscious, reactionary activity and settle into yourself. Eventually meditation will build the habit of mindfulness and this will help you be mindful throughout the day, constantly aware of your thoughts and emotions as they happen.

But to start, take a minute to sit in silence. See how many breaths you can count as you observe your thoughts and emotions without getting sucked in. Only could do five minutes? Good for you! That's enough for today. Do it again tomorrow.

Maybe make it a habit to take a time-out whenever you are stressed or overwhelmed. A few moments of conscious breathing to center yourself before you go back into the action.

So knowing what you know now about meditation and mindfulness, do you see why it's such a crucial part of waking up? We've become so distracted and so identified with being "somebody" that we are so far removed from our truest self.

When you start to identify more with your true self and less with your ego identity, you not only feel more inner peace and happiness, but you are able to create from a more authentic place. One that is truly you. This is the voice that we creators are trying to find. Most do it by trying on different styles and seeing which one "fits" them the most. But why not go straight to the source?

Cultivating Self Knowledge

Self knowledge and awareness is key to a life-changing morning routine. What better way to do this than to write about it daily. The habit of journaling helps you keep track of your progress and also gets your thoughts out of your head.

Unexpressed thoughts and feelings can lead to irritability, anxiety, and depression, not to mention physical sickness.

I tried journaling many times in the past. I would buy a nice notebook and a pen and I'd write my thoughts out with good intentions. My handwriting would start off neat and tidy but by the end of it, I was scribbling my ideas down because I was tired of writing already. I couldn't keep up with my thoughts. This was tiresome and I eventually stopped wanting to write anything because I just didn't like to write.

A year passed and I tried to pick journaling back up. I got a new Moleskine notebook and put it by my bedside. Each night, I'd write down a list of what I did that day. It was pragmatic and utilitarian. It wasn't about expressing emotion or writing letters to myself. It was strictly business!

Even after a few weeks of consistently doing it, I faded. By the time I got to bed, I was already so tired I just didn't feel like doing it. So the journaling habit died again. There was no funeral and nobody cared, so what was the big deal?

Then I remember somewhere in 2011 or 2012 I was feeling like I was having more unhappy days than happy days. It was peculiar and I wasn't sure what was wrong with me. I picked up an app called *MoodKit* and started rating my moods from 1-10 every day and jotting down some notes each time about how I was feeling.

This worked quite a bit because it was a lot faster for me to do. And I could see a graph of my emotional ratings over time and see how up-and-down they were. I also noticed that I did have plenty of good days, I just wasn't paying attention to them. But my bad days were pretty dark and hopeless, which was why I thought I should pay attention in the first place.

But even that habit slowly died, too. I started skipping days and before you know it I wasn't interested. I had moved on to more novel things and I felt like I had got enough information to realize I was depressed. Keeping a mood journal wasn't going to make me any less depressed, I thought.

It wasn't until the summer of 2013 that I even thought about journaling again. At this point I was already six months "out." Meaning, six months after I had told important people in my life I was depressed and trying to get better.

I had been reading lots of stuff about productivity and habits and this is when I started my wake up early habit. And when I read Hal Elrod's book *The Miracle Morning*, he stressed how important it was to keep a journal and document your journey. I must have been convinced by Hal's motivational writing style because I was totally inspired.

He asked if you were a digital or analog person. Do you like typing your journal entries or writing them by hand? Well I already knew writing by hand was getting me nowhere, and I thought by now there had to be a cool journaling app out there.

After a quick search online I found *Day One* for Mac and iOS. I installed it and created my first journal entry. Wow, that was super fun and gratifying. The app is beautifully designed and even has a tagging feature so I can tag every person, place, or thing I write about. This came in handy when I wanted to look back at any times that I was pissed off, cried, felt inspired, or had an out-of-body experience.

I kept posting journal entries and adding photos with my entries.

WHAT TO WRITE ABOUT

Since I was just starting my *Miracle Morning* routine, I was writing about that. I was journaling about how excited I was to get up that morning. I was writing notes about the books I was reading. I think I was reading *The Power of Now* by Eckhart

Tolle at the time and felt like I had an "aha" moment every time I read that book.

I also started the meditation habit, so I would write how the day's meditation went. A typical entry would be like, "Boy, my mind was racing this morning. I couldn't stop thinking. My back hurt after awhile. But I did feel a wave of bliss come over me about halfway through. Then I felt thankful and peaceful. Glad I did it."

After I had my first out-of-body experience, I got really into trying to do it again. I would write about my progress and of course journal as much as I could about what I experienced while out-of-body.

One important thing I do is writing down my dreams every morning. This was key to having more dreams and eventually more lucid dreams. So I had a tag called "dream journal" in Day One and any time I wanted to review I could always click on the tag to see my dreams.

The journaling habit was going great for months. I felt like it was actually easy to keep this one because I could create an entry from my iPhone as well. There were days I skipped on accident, but the next day I could retroactively make an entry on the day I missed and jot down what happened. So then the calendar section wouldn't show I missed a day.

It was a special day when I made it a *full year* of daily journaling. I missed a few days while out of my routine on vacation, but I was OK with that. After a year had gone by, I unlocked this amazing "feature" of being able to see what I wrote exactly one year ago to the day. This was so cool. It's not actually a feature, obviously, but this is one of the benefits of journaling for a year.

I could see how far I had come. I could see how frustrated I was with specific areas in my life and how those don't even bother me today. I could see how inspired I was at the time and then wonder why I never did anything with those ideas. I could see my growth and awakening happen bit by bit.

And the contrast from how I was then with how I was today was refreshing. It brought clarity to my progress that I might not have been able to notice.

So this brings me to the other important aspect of journaling that I don't seem many people talk about. And that is regular reflection. Looking back on your old entries. I never even started doing this until after a year had gone by. But recently I started doing a Sunday Reflection routine.

REGULAR REFLECTION

The Sunday Reflection routine is just a daily task I give myself every Sunday where I look back at my week and create a new journal entry with a summary of my accomplishments, feelings, and realizations I had. It's so important to look back at your accomplishments and feel good about them because that sends a positive message to your brain and body. It's also easy to forget!

It takes me about 30 minutes to look back at the week's entries and jot down my notes about it. I will include a sample after this section.

What else can you journal about besides your thoughts and feelings? Many people journal about what happened that day, but their focus isn't necessarily on growth or self actualization. But for us, it's about aligning ourselves with our true self. It's about self discovery and enlightenment. It's about living a fulfilled life.

Following these suggestions will help you experience realizations, "aha" moments, and paradigm shifts. It will lead to more lucky coincidences and more moments of joy.

ഇൽ

SAMPLE SUNDAY REFLECTION

Did I accomplish my goals from last week?

- set intentions for each day - **yes**
- draw something each day - **maybe half the days**
- record guitars for new song - **done!**
- write four days in book - **3/4 days, but good days**
- finish client's logo - **no, waiting on feedback**
- research guitar lessons - **no, I didn't feel like it**
- quiet the mind practice - **once**

Accomplishments:

- made big strides in my book writing
- recorded and posted a podcast on meditation
- recorded everything for our new song
- bought Superior Drummer from Amazon
- met a friend for a hike and it was fun to be in nature
- got offered to design a vector pack for $350, I'll take it
- uncluttered living room, kitchen, and spare bedroom

Feelings:

- excited over recent email conversations and friendships
- mystical awe, curiosity over nature, faeries, spirits
- distracted and busy on Tues–a "lost" day with errands
- craving coffee, my caffeine detox is hard
- felt sick on fri, sat, and sun
- empowered by possibility of overcoming social anxiety
- nervous/anxious at overcoming social anxiety, scared!
- sad, but loving–our aunt died this week

"Aha" Moments/Takeaways:

- have one exclusive relationship–with *Life itself*
- draw something every day to access inner child
- you can't think your way into your heart
- it's all about taking action
- truth, love, power (mind, heart, balls)
- what you put out into the world, you get back

Goals for this week:

- write four days this week, wrap up first draft
- produce and mix "Distracted" for my band

- stay off coffee for one more week
- catch up on my todo list
- finish client logo design project
- draw a couple days this week
- exercise, go to rec center, and walk outside
- journal my dreams
- stay present, do meditations daily
- wake up early, take action
- practice extroversion, do something that scares me

DEALING WITH NEGATIVE EMOTIONS

We all have negative emotions, and it's just as healthy to journal about those too. You can wrap those negative emotions in a loving and compassionate hug.

You are not your thoughts or feelings, but you are the witness of them. So when you observe yourself feeling angry or worried, you can write about them from the perspective of your observer. Your higher self.

Sometimes it helps to imagine you are talking to your inner child. And the *big you* can hold the space for those negative emotions to fully express themselves. You don't want to suppress or stuff down your negative emotions, that's why it helps so much to journal them. But there will always be a part of you that is outside of that. You can care for your inner child who is experiencing anxiety about what happened at work that day. You can validate your own negative emotions and allow them to exist.

But this new perspective treats negative emotions with love, compassion, and respect. Negative emotions are signals that something is up. And you can use this as a tool to inquire and look within at what might have caused it. This approach to working with negative emotion is a very high vibrational state that resonates love and compassion out into the universe. Attracting more love and compassion your way. The next thing I love to write about is gratitude.

How Gratitude Leads to a Better Life

You may have heard this one before, but if you're like me, you never really got it. After all my research into consciousness, meditation, the nature of reality, and metaphysics - gratitude always seems to come up. Being thankful for what you have. Being thankful for the experiences you had and even for the challenges you faced. Because every challenge is a gateway to learning more about who you are.

I'm going to get deep here and try to communicate why I think gratitude works so well at making us happy. Gratitude is an emotion of appreciation. It's a "high vibrational" emotion like joy and love. Every emotion you feel sends energy outward into the universe. If you imagine an emotion like love being a waveform emanating from your body, it has a certain frequency to it.

Positive emotions, ones that feel good, have a higher frequency. They make you feel open and expansive. Negative emotions like fear, anger, and sadness have a low frequency and those don't feel very good to us. They make us feel closed and contracted.

When you are in a state of gratitude, you are sending out a wave of energy all around you. It's like a note on a piano being played. And it will attract harmonizing notes that sound good with it. I know this is kind of abstract, but stay with me. This is called resonance.

You ever hear someone say, "this article really resonates with me?" That's because it harmonized with their state of being. The music sounded good to them. It was pleasing to the ear. Or in this case, it felt good to them. They read the article and felt more expansive after reading it.

When you emanate these positive emotions, you are in a "high vibration" and you will pay attention to things that resonate with your state of being. You will notice more good things in the world. You will experience more gratitude, love, and joy.

And on the flip side, if you are feeling contracted and fearful, you are still sending an emotional frequency outward. And it will resonate with other like frequencies and draw more negativity to you. This is why people say "misery loves company." Because when you're pissed off, it's not fun being around a person who is happy-go-lucky all the time.

Expressing gratitude will attract more gratitude into your life. It's that simple. The more you appreciate what you have, you will find you will have more. If you are always focused on how little you have, then you are sending that message out to the universe. You will receive resonating energies coming back at you that validate your state of being. So in practical terms, the more you focus on lack, the more lack you receive.

This is what is called the *Law of Attraction*. You may have heard this before. Your thoughts and emotions play a big part in your reality. You are the creator and every thought is a creative thought. Positive or negative, your reality will reflect this.

So gratitude and appreciation for what you have is such a good thing to journal about. But how do you do it?

You can simply write down three things you are grateful for that day. Easy. Things like the food you ate, the roof over your head, the fact that you have electricity, etc. Those are common things to write about. But try to be specific and include events that directly pertain to your self growth. Any time you had an "aha" moment while reading a book, make that something you feel gratitude for.

The common mistake people make when writing a gratitude list is they rush through it. I know I've done this. I just want to get it over with so I can turn off my phone and go to bed. Sure that's nice and all but the message I'm really sending isn't one of gratitude but of obligation, procrastination, and trying to rush.

You see, despite me actually jotting down my gratitude list, my emotional state wasn't actually in a state of gratitude.

While writing my list was a good start, it helps to take a second and actually *feel* the gratitude in your body while you do it. So maybe only jot down one thing and list out a couple reasons why. Then you might start to feel the warmth of appreciation rise up within you. That's when you know you've done it!

If you want to get really good at this, try focusing on that during your meditations. Or try feeling this gratitude in the actual moment that your experience is taking place. Then! If you are feeling it, notice where it is in your body. Probably somewhere near your heart.

Try expanding that feeling throughout your whole body, arms, and legs. See if you can do it by using your thoughts and intention. You might see that you can raise that feeling of appreciation into a swell of emotion.

This is sending a crescendo of positive energy out into the universe. And you know what will happen next? Another person who resonates with that emotion might be tempted to talk to you. Or you might get an email with some good news. Try it! Not only does it feel good when doing it, it has tremendous long term benefits.

You Really are Amazing

When I first heard about doing affirmations, I didn't think much of them. They were positive thinking techniques to help you get out of a funk. I never tried them or put them into practice until I read about them in *The Miracle Morning*.

An affirmation is basically an "I am" statement. You would write down something like, "I am amazing" or "I am worthy of love as I am." The idea is to repeat this consistently every day until it becomes a subconscious belief, and thus true for you.

I always kind of wrote them off as silly self-help techniques, or wishful thinking. But I have since come around and do believe they are powerful tools.

Affirmations are practiced by many successful people. Is it the sole reason why they are successful? Obviously not. But why do they do it?

You see, we are practicing affirmations to ourself all the time. Whether we know it or not. Most of the time our affirmations are negative and self defeating. Common thoughts are, "I'm not good enough" or "I'm never going to get the job I love." And those negative beliefs often become recurring thought loops in your head that constantly repeat themselves.

You know what happens? Those thoughts eventually become reality. They might be true feelings you have. I know that despite all my successes in life, I would always have a tendency to downplay my achievements and minimize my good qualities. I would take pride in my humble nature and say that I didn't think I was that great. Or that I would say I would never be as good as so-and-so.

There would certainly be some bad days where you might go into a negative spiral where these thoughts compound on each other. You might start to see evidence where those feelings come true. You might not get called for that interview, you might get rejected, you might get criticized. And then you will validate those negative beliefs and the cycle continues.

But did you know that the reverse is true? For people who wake up every day and look in the mirror and think positive thoughts, good things tend to happen to them. Or at least, they tend to notice the good things more often than not. To them their positive thoughts become reality.

It works both ways.

So the reason affirmations became such a popular tool in self-improvement circles is because books and movies like *The Secret* marketed them as ways you can "manifest abundance." Meaning, to make a wish upon the universe and finally receive that raise, promotion, new car, or new lover you've been wishing for. Many people started using affirmations like "I am rich. I am wealthy. I am deserving of money" as if they are magic words that will summon the genies of the universe to make your dreams come true.

Now this is true to an extent. This concept became so popular because it seemed so easy. That this is all you had to do. That you could get rich by simply dreaming about it. By repeating positive affirmations with some vague mystical assurance that a $1,000 check would arrive in your mailbox.

And sometimes that does happen. Believe me, it's happened to me! But it wasn't necessarily the result of repeating positive affirmations every day like some sort of ritual.

I actually had a few experiences where I received random large sums of money just "showing up" out of thin air!

My first memory of this was when I received a letter in the mail saying I was owed $23,000 in unpaid royalties for an article I wrote on my company's blog back in 2006. Are you kidding me? Obviously it was a scam, so I just ignored it. Who gets random royalties from a t-shirt design tutorial? Especially when I never signed up for any service that would pay me royalties.

I ignored the letter. A couple months later I received another letter from the same company telling me they had been trying to reach me about these unpaid royalties. My wife told me to look into it.

I brought it to my business partner and he flipped out. We both thought it was some kind of scam, but after reading it, all they required was to fill out a W-9 form so we could get paid. I didn't have to wire money to foreign bank or any weird thing like that.

We thought, what's the worst that could happen? So we called the company and talked to a woman who was about as rational and real as you could get. She told us that our article was being used by an Australian university as part of a graphic design course. Somehow, somebody was paying for usage of this tutorial, but we weren't getting paid. And this woman's job was to get that money into the hands of the original authors.

OK, sounds interesting, but it all seemed too good to be true. We gave her our tax and billing information and in a couple of weeks, we received an actual check for over $23,000! We ended up taking it to the bank to verify it and even called the company with the bank manager to verify everything. They put a hold on the check to make sure everything cleared and sure enough it did. After a few days we had our money and the woman was very happy to help us.

Imagine that.

But I don't remember doing any positive affirmations to make this happen. I do remember actually learning about the Law of Attraction shortly before this all went down. It was mind boggling how this could work.

This is the kind of stuff that people who practice the *Law of Attraction* techniques *hope* for, but might never receive. Simply reciting affirmations or "placing an order with the universe" isn't enough. You have to believe what you write as if it's already true. That's why it's an affirmation, not wishful thinking.

For affirmations to work, they should be reminders of how great you are. Reminders of how you are on track to fulfilling your life's purpose. Reminders that you are good enough as you are. So when you read them back to yourself, you feel good. You actually *feel* an inspired feeling inside you. It might feel like reassurance or relief.

When you read one of your affirmations in the morning and you don't really believe it, you can tell. That just means you need to adjust your affirmations to something more accurate. For example instead of "I love my life" you might say "I am on my path to a life I love."

I had noticed that I felt better when I used positive affirmations as a reminder rather than as a "manifesting tool." I am aware that my thoughts create my reality, so I am careful with how I word my affirmations. If you constantly think, "Success is just around the corner" then that's what you get. A life where success is just around the corner.

You might better write it as, "Success is not something to achieve, but a state of mind. I am successful right here and now. And each day brings new realizations that inspire me in ways I can't yet comprehend."

Can you see the difference in thinking?

After awhile you start to think like this and it becomes unconscious. You start noticing small moments of success like when that person emails you a nice thank you for how much you helped them. Or that smile you received from the grocery store clerk. Or when you made your nephew laugh with that silly dance you did. Then you start to see how success really is formed.

Affirmations are little reminders that you can repeat every day that train your brain out of the negative thinking patterns it has become accustomed to.

These negative thought patterns are not our fault. We're bombarded with messages that we aren't good enough. Every advertising message is trying to tell you that you aren't good enough as you are and that their product will make you better. Heck, it's nearly impossible to market something without first pointing out the problem and trying to convince people they have it.

When you use some of the habits in this book to become more mindful and aware of your thoughts and emotions, you can spot these self-defeating ideas in their tracks. Once you do, you can reverse it.

Next time you catch yourself worrying or having anxiety about your future, stop yourself. And then think about the opposite. Think about the most relieving thought you can have. Notice how you are projecting into the future and imagining a scenario in which you do not have enough. What if you could reverse that?

This is a great way to come up with your own affirmations. Your own affirmations will make you feel alive, inspired, open, and expansive. They will come from a deep-seeded desire to be loved and live a fulfilled life. At our core that's what most of us crave.

For me personally, I use the Notes app on my iPhone to write down any new affirmations. And most days I open that up and read some of them. They are little inspirational thoughts that I had that I am reminding myself of.

Sometimes they get old and no longer apply. If you find yourself reading them and it doesn't feel fresh or have any "juice" left in it, then it might be time to revise it.

Another technique is recording your own audio affirmations. I haven't done this yet, but I want to try it. I saw a guy on YouTube suggest it. He said that listening to your own voice remind you that you are loved and accepted for who you are, or are on your path to an amazing life, is extremely powerful.

He said he records this on his phone and then listens to it while he works out. This might sound silly, but man, I bet you it's effective! If this is too much for you, that's OK.

Maybe the old trick of looking into the mirror, directly into your eyes, and giving a nod of approval. Saying, "you got this" is all you need.

Move Your Body

We all know how important exercise is to our well-being and physical health. Everyone is trying to get fit, lose ten pounds, or tone up.

But admittedly, exercise has been the most difficult habit for me. Most of the time I've tried to work out, I just can't get into it! I'm lucky to be as slim as I am, because the sedentary lifestyle I live as a designer and writer is not conducive to a sculpted body.

I have a bone to pick with exercise. I'm just going to get this off my chest. We are sold this idea of having this ideal body. Many of us these days work at a desk. Sitting for the majority of the day. We come home from our office job and sit some more.

Almost all of our activities involve sitting and interacting with a glowing screen. And we're sold food and beverages that make us fat and diabetic. And then there exists an industry that claims to have the solution, the fitness industry.

Gyms are hilarious to me. It's like a giant cage with hamster wheels for humans. And most of the reasons why we work out are based on guilt and fear. We feel bad about ourselves and feel like we need to adhere to some idealized standard. Men must have six-pack abs and women must look good in those leggings!

I know some people enjoy working out. It's a physical release. We need it! Because most of our jobs these days are mental, we crave some sort of physical activity. I've tried gym memberships, personal trainers, and workout apps. But none of them have been able to stick with me. Working out just doesn't inspire me, I have to say.

However, I do love to dance and play. I enjoy sweating my ass off playing drums in my band for two hours each week. For years I took breakdance classes because the hard labor of training felt justified by the cool moves I was learning. And the music drove me to move. I wasn't motivated by vanity or guilt, but passion!

I have no problem sweating and straining my body. But when I'm on a treadmill or lifting weights, I can't seem to summon enthusiasm. Maybe you can relate?

This is why I have a love/hate relationship with exercise. You see, after 32 years of life, I firmly believe that I'm an artist at heart. A creator.

WAKE UP

My head is in the clouds half the time and I'm dreaming of new ideas, new songs, and new projects. I used to be a big film buff and lately I've become a voracious reader. I'm also somewhat of a technology geek and I do admit I get excited about things that keep me glued to a glowing screen.

So if I am being honest, exercise just doesn't come naturally to me. But playing does. When I was a kid I loved playing football and basketball, but I hated hauling logs and mowing the lawn. Boooring!

Interestingly, I had a psychological horoscope done on myself that shed some light on this problem. It was a 60-page report about my life and my purpose based on how the planets and stars were aligned when I was born. It even described in detail how boring and uninterested I would be in physical and "mundane" matters. That my head is indeed in the clouds and I'm deeply connected to the unseen world. And it takes great effort to ground me into physical reality.

So you see why I might have a problem running on the treadmill at a gym?

But I still do it. I still make the time. Not every day, but it's an effort that I put in. And I usually feel great about it. It's a triumph for me. I can read 300 pages about *The Holographic Universe*, but running three miles is such a chore!

I did get inspired when I took a Yoga class for the first time. It was like break dancing in slow motion! And there were cool moves to learn, I felt like I could level up and contort my body in creative ways. I was more excited about doing handstands than doing yet another downward dog!

One thing that attracted me to Yoga was how the instructor presented it. It was raw, without the fashion of today's modern day Yoga scene. My instructor April was a purist and an idealist, a lot like me. Her calming energy was refreshing and it really brought me back to Earth in a comforting way. I was there to reconnect with my spirit through my body.

At the time I took her classes, I didn't know anything about spirituality and didn't understand many of the words she used. I just knew I felt calm and content after leaving her class.

This was the beginning of my understanding of what physical exercise can do for a person like me. It can ground me. It can calm me down. There's a definite sense of release and relief after a good Yoga session. It's not the hardcore feeling of accomplishment after one of the workouts I had with a personal trainer, but a more satisfying and emotional connection with my body and the Earth. But I didn't know that at the time. Such concepts were foreign to me. I was still focused on achieving advanced poses or not looking dumb in front of other people.

I ended up getting too busy to take her classes. I tried doing yoga at home to videos or apps, but it just didn't feel the same. I started to feel like I was working out for working out's sake. I felt like I was just in a different hamster wheel, except it looked more like a yoga mat. I fell out of the habit.

Around November of 2014 I received an email from a naturopathic doctor Dr. Jody Stanislaw. She was also a life coach, which was inspiring at the time because I had just started coaching people about morning routines. We agreed to coach each other toward our goals.

She asked me the area of my life I wanted to improve. Naturally I felt like exercise was high on my list, so we went with it. What Jody told me about exercise is something I'll never forget.

She said a workout is less about perspiration than it is determination. The physical exertion portion is only 25% of the battle. The other 75% is self-discipline. She said a workout is a "personal triumph over laziness and procrastination."

Boom. It hit me.

When you workout regularly, your emotional problems diminish, your confidence grows, and your spirit toughens. Procrastination and laziness plagued me when it came to physical exercise.

When she reframed exercise in that way, I felt inspired. The "get a firm body" message never resonated with me. I remember reading an article about the "death of masculinity" that said since many men are office workers these days, they have to resort to putting on "show muscles" to preserve their idea of masculinity. I felt like that statement had some truth to it.

Jody also stated how important it is to simply *move your body*. It doesn't matter how much you can bench press or how far you can run. What matters is that you are greasing your wheels and not getting rusty. When we sit all day, our muscles in our legs atrophy. Our backs get hunched over and we slowly but surely develop poor posture and put on extra weight around our bellies.

But even that isn't the point. Our bodies are representative of the lifestyle we live. If our lifestyle is sedentary, our body adapts. If our jobs are to be creative thinkers and innovators, we strengthen our minds and our spirits, but our bodies somehow get forgotten. In an increasingly digital world where most of our work is done on computers, it's no wonder our physical bodies get soft.

The thing that really sold me on exercise was it's ability to ground me in physical reality. As I have said before, my head is in the clouds a lot of the time. For a lot of us creative thinkers, we are chronically ungrounded.

BEING GROUNDED ON EARTH

But what does that even mean? I had a hard time understanding this concept of grounding. Carla Fox, a shamanic and quantum sphere healer, told me that she doesn't think I've been grounded for much of my whole life.

What?

I asked Gigi Young, another spiritual coach of mine, about grounding. What does it mean and how does it feel?

"All creativity and inspirations must move through our higher consciousness down into our most basic material expression here on Earth. This is what makes an idea grounded. It means that it has made it through the percolation process of the human consciousness and is being expressed in a "grounded" way where the paradigms of the collective 3D world are considered and used." – Gigi Young

In other words, she said that grounding is simply taking the energy that comes in to us through inspiration and ideas and grounding it into physical reality. Taking your brilliant ideas and making them happen in reality.

Put another way, it's like electricity. The wires needs to be grounded otherwise it could explode.

For us, our ideas, thoughts, and emotions are energy. They are often swimming around in our heads. Emotions, for example might be stuck in parts of our body like our chest or our stomach. We might feel that tightening in our solar plexus when we feel worried about something. And repetitive thoughts race through our minds. Inspiring ideas come and go but unless we do something about it, they escape us.

Grounding means getting all of that energy out of us. When we do, we feel relaxed, calm, content, and peaceful. For example, have you ever had a list of a million things to do running through your head? What happens when you decide to write them down on a piece of paper? You feel a little bit of relief. What you've done is to ground some of that energy and it feels good to release it.

RELEASING BLOCKED ENERGY

Gigi said that we all go through these cycles of inspiration–thoughts–manifestation. In other words, we get an idea, then we think about that idea. It's possibilities forming in our mind and eventually the urge to take action arises and we manifest our thought in physical reality. This is the process of creation.

Many people feel anxious or depressed when their ideas never come to fruition. When they are unable to express their thoughts or emotions, they cause stress, anxiety, and depression. There are many reasons why someone wouldn't be able to manifest their ideas. A big one is fear and limiting beliefs. They talk themselves out of it, they are afraid of what people will think, they suppress their inspired desires because they don't know how to make it a reality.

After this discussion with Gigi, I felt like I finally understood what grounding meant. I started writing a list of things that ground me. On that list was physical exercise, walking, dancing, playing music, having sex, cooking food, doing chores, being outside in nature, etc.

I remember when I used to have my break dance classes right after work. I would come into class feeling stressed and anxious. Maybe even worried about my projects or future. And after an intense class, I would leave feeling totally centered and content. Relieved. Sure I was a sweaty mess and my body hurt, but I felt like my mental stress was gone. I believe that was because there was a lot of pent-up energy in my mind and body. And this physical exercise was how it was released.

Not only did I release the pent-up energy, I also triumphed over laziness and procrastination. Not to mention learning a new move! Talk about worth it! Suddenly my problems didn't seem so big anymore. My insecurities seemed to disappear, at least for the time being.

Exercise is so important, especially for creative people like us. We spend so much time on computers and media that we are overloaded with stimulation. Daily walks, yoga, or workouts help alleviate this.

As I write this, exercise is still something I struggle with. I hope to change that.

There was one more thing that Dr. Jody told me that has helped me build an exercise habit. Do not start out with huge goals or ambitions! You will get burned out. You might even be nodding your head as you probably have started and stopped different habits like this yourself.

She said just start out with the tiniest version of your workout. I told her I'd go to the local rec center three times per week. She said that was too much, just go once per week. And it didn't matter what I did there, I just had to go.

I had to show up. And that's the triumph over laziness and procrastination she was talking about. Just showing up. That's the 75% determination. The other stuff is easy.

I hope that you add exercise into your routine. Just a little each day. On the days you aren't working out, go for a walk. Do some jumping jacks and some stretching. Grease those wheels! Turn on some music and dance. Find an adult sports league where everyone kind of sucks and it's more about fun than being good. Move your body in some way.

Don't stay glued to your computer for goodness' sakes! Don't work out for fear-based motivations such as guilt or shame.

Feel the relief of releasing your pent-up energy. Relish in the achievement of overcoming procrastination simply by showing up. And take it one day at a time. Start small and only add more if you want to.

Now if you'll excuse me, I've been sitting here writing for over two hours, I need to move my body!

CHAPTER FOUR

OVERCOMING CHALLENGES

By now you understand what it takes to build a life-changing morning routine. But there will be obstacles and challenges you must overcome.

I know from my own experience as well as my coaching clients, that what follows are solutions to the most common problems people face when waking up early. After this, you should have no excuse!

හෝ

I'm Not a Morning Person

Many of us believe that there are such things as being a "morning person" or a "night owl." Do some people just have that early-riser gene? Maybe that's the case. Maybe some people *do* naturally wake up early without a big fuss. They rise naturally with the sun and go to bed early.

But not me, I was a night owl through-and-through. Was it in my nature? Maybe. But I *learned* to become an early riser. I taught myself how to do it. I read about it. I practiced. I made mistakes and messed up. But I got better each day.

You may have uttered the phrase "I'm not a morning person" at some time in your life. You are implying that you are unable to wake up early. You are identifying yourself as the opposite of someone who gets up early. That's like saying "I'm not a 'gym rat'" or "I'm not a 'health nut.' "

You are implying that the "morning person," "gym rat," or "health nut" are types of people and you just can't relate. It makes it hard to get into the habit when you feel that way. This is the identification problem.

THE IDENTIFICATION PROBLEM

When I first went to the gym, I was intimidated. I didn't want to go, but my girlfriend dragged me along. There were loads of people there on these weird looking machines. Many had cool, fancy workout clothes. There were many attractive people there who seemed to know what they were doing. I was definitely not one of those people. I was a nerdy art student who wanted to work out, but I didn't fit in. I felt like a fish out of water.

The problem was that I was doing the whole "identification" thing. I was creating me vs. them mentality. I was separating myself from everyone else. My sense of self did not include going to the gym. I was more comfortable in front of a drawing desk or computer screen. I had a hard time convincing myself to go.

117

I went three times and that was it. I forgot to mention I signed a two-year contract with a $50 per month membership fee. I couldn't cancel it. So even the negative reinforcement of losing all that money wasn't enough to get me to go to the gym.

A few years later I noticed I was pretty out of shape. I didn't want to go to the gym again. I decided to try to find a personal trainer, someone I could go to privately to help me get in shape without having to "look the part." My biggest request of them was to help me change my mindset to someone who works out. It didn't take long for me to start feeling this way after three rigorous workouts per week. I did that for a few months before I started to feel bored.

I was ready to go out and do my own thing. I signed up at the local rec center and started taking break dance classes. I began to see myself as someone who took exercise more seriously. And my perception of people who went to gyms started to become more realistic. They are people just like me. Young and old, of all body types. They also probably feel the same level of social anxiety as well. I started to feel more comfortable and actually eager to work out.

How this translates to the whole "night owl" vs. "morning person" thing is that it boils down to your sense of self. When you strongly believe you are a certain way, it's going to be hard to change. You have to give up the identification of either side. You are not one or the other. You are fluid. You can become anything you desire.

It's important that you get rid of this mental bias. Those you call "morning people" would likely feel the same about "night owls." But if you really want to carve out time and become an early-riser, you need to change the way you think about yourself.

You can think of yourself as a person who changes things. A person who experiments with life.

When we say "I am not a 'morning person,'" that's an affirmation. You could just as easily say "I am a 'morning person.'" If that doesn't feel right, say "I'm on my way to becoming a 'morning person.'"

One cool thing about identifying with a role is that you are able to stick to the habits better. When you start to associate a particular habit with your sense of self, it becomes a lot harder to change. So use this judiciously. Don't ever get too stuck on identifying with a particular role you play, whether it's a "morning person," "night owl," "gym rat," "health nut," mother, father, etc. Those are roles we play, not who we really are. You can play with identities and notice how it affects your motivation levels. It can be fun. But always keep yourself grounded and centered.

Not Enough Time

Probably the biggest excuse people give me for not waking up early is they don't have time. Even if they *want* to wake up early, they believe it's impossible. We all have 24 hours in a day and we all have free will to change things. It's just our fears and limiting beliefs that get in the way. We believe we do not have free will. We believe if we changed we would upset our stable routine, rock the boat, upset others, or make life more difficult.

I totally understand *all* of those reasons. I sympathize with those who have lots of obligations and a busy schedule. At some point you chose, allowed, or let in all of those obligations. The only person that can do anything about it is you.

When we say we don't have time, it's not in reference to waking up early. It's usually to things like meditating, reading, journaling, exercising, etc. All those happy habits we know are good for us are the things we say we don't have time for. We are too busy to sit down for five minutes to meditate. I know that sounds crazy: that someone could be so busy that finding five minutes of silence is too difficult.

When you put it that way, it seems like anyone could take a few minutes to sit and be still. Usually this logic is enough to get me to start a habit. I did this. I meditated for five minutes during the day as a break from my busy schedule. But sooner or later, I just got busy and "never found the time" to fit it in. It wasn't that I didn't actually *have* five minutes, it's that I didn't know how to fit it in. It just wasn't convenient. There was always something else to be done.

When I did have time, I didn't feel like meditating, I wanted to scroll through social media or busy myself with something entertaining. Sitting in silence may have sounded nice, but I didn't see the point. It wasn't fun.

But you see that "I don't have time" is an excuse. It's frustrating to try to fit habits into in our busy schedules. So that's why I started waking up early. To *make* time. To carve out time. I was willing to sacrifice my sleep to do it. I knew I'd eventually settle into a regular sleep habit at some point. It was so important to me to make time.

By waking up early, you carve out time on purpose for yourself. Now you finally have the time to do those things you've always wanted. This sounds so easy! Now, don't go reaching for that "I don't have time" excuse! We all know it's a lie.

But you don't know that it's a lie yet. If this sounds like where you are, try taking a look at what you do during a typical day. How much of it is spent on things you really want to do? How much of it is spent doing things you don't? Wouldn't you want to take a step toward shifting this in your favor? Start to get a sense of how much time you feel is "wasted" on doing things that don't add value to your life.

Lots of us are in the habit of pleasing other people before ourself. And the "I don't have time" excuse is almost like saying, "I'm not allowed." There's a deep fear of displeasing other people if you take time for yourself. The only thing you can do is try it. Take some time for yourself in small increments to see that you do in fact have the time. *You need to give yourself permission.* You get to decide how your 24 hours of a day will be spent, not anyone else.

The Willpower Problem

When we attempt a waking-early habit, the hardest thing to do is get out of bed. When you think about it, it's not hard at all. We've done way harder things in our life. We've started businesses, won championships, given birth and raised children. But getting out of bed seems like the impossible task sometimes!

There's a little thing called inertia. When an object is in motion, it stays in motion. When an object is at rest, it stays at rest. You've been resting for several hours and are transitioning out of sleep. You are warm and cozy in your blankets. It's dark outside still. You don't want to get up! You just want to keep sleeping.

I know. Boy do I know. This is one of the hardest things to deal with. When we're laying there telling ourselves to get up when the rest of us just wants to stay put, we're at a crossroads. If we try to talk ourselves into it, we might find ourselves talking ourselves <u>out</u> of it instead. Our mental capacity is really low when we wake up. It takes an extreme amount of willpower to force ourselves out of bed in this way.

This is where many people will start talking about self-discipline. And if we're unable to do it, we beat ourselves up inside. We try to use a drill sergeant technique. We try to boss around our bodies and think of how much of a failure we'll be if we don't do get up. There can be a downward spiral of negative self-talk if you let yourself lay there and debate in your bed.

The new trend is a twist on self-discipline. It's reducing the need for willpower by establishing habits and routines.

Willpower is a finite resource. The more we use up in the beginning of the day, the less we have later until we are able to recharge. We want to be able to use our willpower to muster up courage to do our important tasks that move us closer to our goals and aspirations. Not waste it all before we get out of bed.

So how *do* we turn getting out of bed into a habit? The trick is to not think about it.

DON'T LET YOURSELF THINK!

The more you can plan out the night before, the better. Make sure you know exactly what you are going to do when you get up so there's no thinking about it. Know your trigger, routine, reward sequence. Trigger: alarm goes off. Routine: get out of bed, turn it off. Reward: cup of coffee, TV show, hot shower, etc. Whatever you want to make it.

Know your morning routine before you go to bed. You have to know you are going to make progress on your habits. You are going to be one step closer to your goals. You have to know *The Slight Edge* is in effect. "Just a little every day" is key. Knowing this before you go to bed will help you avoid the mental exercise of searching for a reason to get up.

Another tip is to set out your clothes for the next day the night before. If you work out in the morning, put your workout clothes and shoes by your bed. It's ready and waiting for you so you don't have to think about it.

And lastly, the biggest "hack" is putting the alarm across the room. One of my coaching clients even suggested putting the alarm in the kitchen with the volume turned way up. He'd have to run out into the kitchen to turn it off in the morning. I thought that was hilarious and a great idea. I haven't tried it myself yet.

The alarm across the room is the most effective way to *get out of bed* in the morning. It's also the most jarring. Once you are out of bed, you are less likely to go back to sleep. There have been times I was low on willpower and inspiration and went to the couch and fell asleep again. But that is rare.

So remember that willpower is a resource you should use wisely. Do what you can to reduce the need for willpower. And remember, don't let yourself think!

I'm Too Tired!

If you find yourself simply too tired in the morning, it's a sign that you're not getting enough sleep. Either that, or your sleep quality is not good. How much sleep are you getting each night? Is there a way you can modify your routine to get enough sleep?

While carving out time for your epic morning routine is important, we don't want to sacrifice our sleep for too long. We will get burned out. When we first wake up we are at our sleepiest. If you use the alarm across the room, you immediately wake up a little bit more just by getting out of bed and standing up.

In my case, I might slowly walk to my dresser and stand there for a minute as I begin to wake up a little. I might be dizzy or groggy. I try to remember if I was dreaming anything and write it in my journal app on my phone. I get my clothes ready for my shower and do all of this while still sleepy.

There is a good chance I'll have some repetitive thoughts going on in my head that are urging me to go back to sleep or to give up. And I often have to just ignore those if I know that my heart's desire is out there waiting for me. I struggled with going back to bed a lot under the belief that I should "listen to my body." Well, that's true to some extent. But our bodies are so much more powerful and capable than we realize. It's our thoughts that often dictate what our bodies are willing to do for us.

If our mindset is pumped and ready for action, our bodies will respond and kick into gear for us. But if our minds lose track of what's important or we continually try to talk ourselves out of doing what we want, our bodies will also respond in kind.

One piece of advice, don't overdo it. If you are forcing yourself up and out of bed on four to five hours of sleep or less, you might be doing more harm than good. Try to recognize whether you are legitimately fatigued or just suffering from typical morning grogginess. Sometimes the grogginess wears off as we put our bodies in motion. Remember, an object in motion stays in motion and an object at rest stays at rest. It's inertia and momentum.

The most important thing is that you are in a process of figuring this out for yourself. This is where being mindful and paying attention to your urges, habits, and motivations come into play. All the habits that I write about in this book will help you discern whether you really need a break or are just procrastinating. And it's OK if you mess up, just keep your eye on the prize. Rest up and get back to it the next day.

Snooze Addiction

Do you have a habit of hitting snooze over and over again before you finally get up? What's your emotional state when you do actually get up? What thoughts are going through your head? Something like, "Ugh, I really don't want to get out of bed. I'm so tired. Do I have to?"

WAKE UP

I admit, I love the snooze button. Because when the alarm goes off, I just want to turn off the noise and keep sleeping. It just became a habit.

What's the danger of hitting snooze? Well, I don't know if I'd call it a danger, but it starts the day off by procrastinating. It doesn't feel like much but this is exactly what we are doing when we hit snooze.

We are opting for just a few more minutes of rest, because we are putting off what's uncomfortable. The sleep we do actually get is broken and unsatisfying. And it's accompanied by some self talk that's usually not so good.

The sure-fire way to prevent snoozing is to use the alarm-across-the-room technique. When it goes off, you have no choice but to get out of bed to stop the noise. And while I know that this is not pleasant, you end up doing it without thinking. When you are standing up out of your bed, you are more likely to stay out and not go back to sleep.

The trick to all of this is to *get up* and *stay up* after the alarm goes off once. This way you are not starting the day of by procrastinating. The pain of not hitting snooze will lessen over time and this will become a habit. Trust me, it gets better! And it works easier if you know what you are going to do right after you turn off your alarm.

I've used this method for a year now and it's worked great. But there are times when I did purposely blow off my morning routine and crawl back into bed. But those times are few and far between. Recently I tried using the *Sleep Cycle* app on my iPhone which requires you to put the phone under your pillow. To snooze all you have to do is move the phone! This is dangerous, because it makes it so easy to keep falling for those brief moments of lousy sleep that only seem satisfying because you are avoiding something else.

So I stopped using *Sleep Cycle* despite the fact that I love seeing my "sleep quality." It just wasn't worth sabotaging myself with the snooze button.

Do I ever hit snooze anymore? Sometimes. I'm not a superhuman. Like I said, I'm still a sucker for hitting the snooze every now and then. But I no longer do this every day like I used to.

So if you want to stop hitting snooze, move your alarm across the room or into a different room.

How Much Sleep Do I Really Need?

Sleep is something you can't avoid discussing when trying to wake up early. But carving out an epic morning routine, you generally will sacrifice some sleep to do it. At first.

When I read *The Miracle Morning*, the author stressed heavily that the amount of sleep you need is largely set by your own expectations. If you believe that you absolutely need eight hours of sleep, than anything less won't work for you. You might wake up feeling tired and groggy. But if you firmly believe that six hours is all you need to feel energized and refreshed, chances are you will wake up feeling energized and refreshed.

He said that when you go to bed, try to tell yourself how excited you will be for the morning. Look at the clock and calculate how many hours of sleep you'll get and then tell yourself that it's exactly the amount of time you'll need to feel refreshed. These positive affirmations will go a long way in convincing your body to play along.

I tried this and it did work. I mean, there have been many times when I was excited about something and got very little sleep. I woke up the next day and still had energy and enthusiasm. I had no trouble waking up. And there were times when I couldn't sleep and knew I was only getting two or three hours of sleep. No matter what I told myself, I was still dead tired the next day.

If you are getting five or less hours of sleep, you should be cautious. You are walking a fine line. Some people rely on coffee and stimulants to get them through the day, thinking that four to five hours of sleep is plenty. This is justified by saying "many successful people get five or less hours of sleep a night." It's not telling the whole story.

Some of my coaching clients brought up how important sleep was. That after awhile it was easy to get burned out. They would crash and burn and oversleep, which can negatively affect your energy levels. This will happen if you carve out a morning routine but don't adjust your bed time.

So how much sleep do you really need?

My life coach Dr. Jody Stanislaw firmly believes that sleep is crucial for good health. She gets at least eight hours every night. For someone who wakes up at 6 a.m., that would mean going to bed at 10 p.m. or earlier. That has always been really hard for me. I am someone who used to go to bed at 2 or 3 a.m. And getting to bed before midnight is hard enough for me!

At my peak, I went for months with getting six or so hours of sleep per night. I did drink coffee twice a day and had a nap after dinner. So I think I was able to get by pretty well. This may be OK for you or it might not be.

Some people really believe they need a lot of sleep. Other people devalue sleep and think it's a waste. You may have heard the phrase "I'll sleep when I'm dead."

I used to be one of those people who thought sleep was a waste. It was a sign that the day was ending. I was attached to my days so much that sleep felt like I was closing the door. I didn't want to let go and I always had something else to do. This was before I started getting up early and actually looking forward to my morning routines.

And we can't forget about the importances of dreams. We are taught in modern Western culture that dreams are basically meaningless. But everything I've discovered since my awakening is quite the contrary. Dreams can tell us so much about ourselves in a way that nothing else can. When we sleep, our bodies are not only recharging physically, but mentally and spiritually as well. The more we sleep, the more our body is tapped into our higher consciousness. It helps us process everything we've learned.

That's why I'm a big proponent of naps. One of the easiest ways to help any lack of sleep you may get from carving out a morning routine is to take a nap during the day. I generally do this after dinner. And now that I'm freelancing and working from home, I do this in the afternoon. It's a great way to reset instead of switching directly to another task.

Sleep is important folks. You need as much as you believe you do.

Bedtime Matters

This book is about morning routines, right? So why are we talking about nighttime routines? I've found that this topic inevitably comes up as people get into the waking early habit. It's generally a result of not getting enough sleep so their bedtime needs to be dialed back.

When you first carve out your morning routine schedule, it's like taking a chunk out of your sleep. You will be getting less sleep when you start. But what I've found is that my bedtime will eventually shift as well. Going from a 2 a.m. bed time and waking up at 6 a.m. is going to be difficult if you are used to getting up at 9 or 10.

It took some getting used to. The initial high of doing my epic morning routine helped me out in the beginning. But naturally my bed time shifted to 1 a.m., then 12:30 a.m., and then midnight.

This had the side effect of inconveniencing my marriage. My wife and I no longer were going to bed at the same time. She wasn't willing to shift her bedtime schedule to fit with my new routine. But eventually we settled into a routine that worked for both of us.

I mention this because I understand that changing our routines affects others around us. And it's good to be aware of this and talk it out with anyone we live with.

So what does a good nighttime routine look like?

Think of it like a bookend. You have your mornings and your nights. And in between is the meat of your day. A lot of our personal happiness depends on how we start and end our days.

At night, I like to wind down. This is becoming a trend amongst creative thinkers I know. We are so digitally connected that spending time "off-screen" at night is critical to our well-being. It helps us settle down. Checking email in bed is probably not helping us become happier people.

So avoid looking at glowing screens 30 minutes before bed time. This is sometimes more difficult than it sounds, especially if we rely on our smartphones to wake us up. Or if we like to watch TV to wind down from our days, or flip through social media before bed. Some people use an app like F.Lux to simulate daylight on their devices.

In my opinion, we are not doing this consciously, but out of habit. If you can observe your tendencies, you can choose how you spend your nights. Treat it like a ritual. Make it sacred.

Read a paper book at night. Write in your journal. Meditate for a little bit. Spend time with family. Do your bathroom ritual slowly and with mindfulness.

And then make sure you have your next morning planned out in advance. Do you know what you will be doing? Eventually this will become a habit and you won't have to remember to do this. Set out anything you need for a better wake-up experience. This will help!

When I crawl into bed these days I feel so much gratitude and joy. It's a far cry from feeling a bleak sense of giving up on the day or having tasks left unfinished. I credit my morning routine for transforming my emotional state at night.

I tried to practice gratitude before bed by writing in my journal. I would think of the good things that happened that day and write them down. I'd make a note of what I liked about myself, what I've learned, what I want to change. It transformed how I feel about nighttime now.

When I go to bed, I feel like I'm coming back "home." Home to my higher self, my inner child, and all of me. And I feel like saying "thank you!" to everyone in the universe. This combined with my comfy mattress, sheets, and pillows, I LOVE going to bed.

On days when I am feeling contracted or worried, I use this time to look inward and connect with my inner child. My inner child is the part of me that hasn't grown up yet. The one is scared of change or worries over things that my higher self knows will be OK.

I have a mental and heart-centered conversation with myself and it's something very personal. Even on bad days I still look forward to going to bed. Lately I've been trying to remember my dreams so I'll make a conscious intention to remember them.

I'll also affirm my intention for the next morning. Something like, "So tomorrow, I'm waking up at 6:30 a.m., I'm going to get up right away and eat breakfast while I watch the next episode of that show I like, then I'll use the next hour to do my happy habits. Sounds good!"

Your bedtime routine will take shape naturally. But you should start thinking about how to make it a nice complement to your mornings.

Brain Fog and Grogginess

When we first wake up, our minds are still adjusting to waking consciousness. We likely woke from a dream and it's hard to get adjusted. I actually enjoy this foggy state of mind because it only happens once a day or so. It's a unique transitional state from sleeping to wakefulness and often accompanied by residual memories from our dreams. This is absolutely normal.

This groggy state might also be accompanied by doubtful self-talk that tries to convince us to go back to bed. But stay with it. Be with the brain fog! Watch it clear up as your wakefulness increases as you move about. Like I said, having brain fog in the mornings is perfectly normal.

I would be concerned if this brain fog continued throughout your routine and into your day. This might be a sign that you are too tired and need some rest. Again, how much sleep are you getting? Are you trying to do too much? Are you bored and need to shake things up again? Lots of times, excitement and enthusiasm go a long way to clearing up prolonged brain fog.

Brain fog prevents us from thinking clearly. Our problem solving ability is hindered and when we're trying to work, this is not a fun state of mind to be in. A cup of coffee might help us temporarily alleviate these symptoms, but the natural way to work through it is to make sure you are getting enough sleep and remembering to stay inspired and fresh.

Staying inspired and fresh simply means making the necessary changes to your routine that are in line with what makes you happy. What are you excited about? Make sure you're keeping your routine updated regularly so you don't fall into a rut. Ruts are where our enthusiasm runs dry and we start to go through our routine without a clear direction or purpose.

Remember, the foggy brain state is interesting and it will clear up as we move about. Be present with it and don't try to expect your mental engines to start right up. Allow it to come online naturally. Avoid the temptation to criticize yourself. Embrace it and recognize it as a unique state of consciousness that's part of our mornings!

How to Kill Procrastination

One of the biggest problems I face is procrastination. Although some would look at all that I have done, and wonder how I could have that problem. Because I seem to get stuff done. But the truth is, I like to put stuff off. I tend to delay the hard work. I'm getting better though.

When I am faced with a decision to do what I know is important to me vs. what feels good in the moment, I will often choose the latter. And this is where self-discipline comes into play.

My intuitive coach Gigi Young said, "Discipline is choosing between what you want now and what you want most." Except most of us don't realize we actually have a choice there. We know the things we have to get done during the day but we often like to do the easy and unimportant stuff first.

How many of you start the day by checking social media, email, or other lightweight tasks? How much time and effort do you spend working toward the things you really want in life?

For me, I do love spending time on what I really want. And that's why I think I've noticed this problem of procrastination come up a lot for me. I'm hyper aware of what I'm doing with my time and I can tell when I'm procrastinating. I can feel the resistance to working.

How do you know if you're procrastinating? What does it feel like? It usually feels like a strong resistance or repelling force. Usually accompanied by feelings of discomfort, unease, or guilt.

Procrastination comes in many forms. It's a symptom of a deeper issue. Sometimes it comes from a deep unconscious fear. Perhaps you are afraid that you aren't good enough. Procrastination is settling for what's comfortable right now. This is a trap to be weary of.

Sure, it's more fun to watch TV and eat potato chips than it is to work out or write your novel. This goes back to that quote about choosing what you want most and not what you want now.

Now that I am working for myself from home, procrastination is an even bigger issue for me. Because I don't have someone else waiting for me. It's all up to me. I am able to gain greater clarity on why exactly I procrastinate.

WHY DO WE PROCRASTINATE?

Perfectionism
We can be perfectionists and we won't start something because we feel it has to be perfect. And anything less than perfect isn't good enough

so we never start or finish that big task. The trick to overcoming perfectionism is to lower your standards by 10-20%. You don't need to do it perfectly. In fact, your 90% is probably better than most people's 100% because you have such high standards.

Too Big of a Task

If the job is too big, like writing a novel or losing 50 pounds, we feel intimidated by it. When I think of writing a whole book, I don't want to start. But when I think of writing a paragraph about procrastination, I suddenly feel more motivated to start. Break down big tasks into baby steps that feel more manageable.

Uncomfortability

Sometimes the task at hand feels uncomfortable. That's why we are avoiding it in the first place. When I think about working out, I feel like it's going to be uncomfortable and I will get sweaty. That thought is enough to derail me! This feeling goes away when I'm playing team sports or dancing with others as my mind is focused on something else. But when you stop focusing on the parts you don't like, try focusing on the parts you *do* like.

Distractions

We know the task at hand is important. But we let distractions get in the way because they are more shiny and delicious than the work we have to do. Imagine if you're trying to eat healthy and people around you keep eating sweets and cheeseburgers! Imagine if they kept offering it to you over and over? That's like trying to focus while simultaneously getting notifications on our phones, emails, and social media accounts. Turn those off! Remove yourself from distractions so you aren't tempted at all.

Feels Like Work

After the initial buzz wears off on a new goal, it starts to feel like work. Work is generally defined as the stuff we do that isn't fun, but we have to do it. This is where we will face the resistance and urge to procrastinate. It helps to constantly remind ourselves of our desired goal. Keep your eye on the prize! Try to find what you like about the task itself. Try to see if you can make the task fun or use a new tool or app to make it fresh. Add some novelty back into the task by working somewhere new, wearing some new gym clothes, lowering the bar a bit, or finding some friends to help you.

Unclear Where to Start

Another reason why we procrastinate is because we are unclear on what needs done. Say we have a big project we know we must complete. It feels daunting and thinking about it causes anxiety. We don't even know where to start, so we avoid it. Over time we feel guilty for not having done what we wanted.

Don't Feel Like it

A common phrase that we used as kids when our parents told us to do chores, "I don't feel like it." Or "But I don't wanna!" That's our inner six-year-old self complaining about hard work. We naturally just want to live free and have fun. This kind of sums up all of the above reasons why we procrastinate. Because in the end, we just don't feel like doing what we have to do! Even if we chose the assignment ourselves.

MY CONFUSION WITH PROCRASTINATION

When I started learning "follow your joy" as a path to a meaningful and happy life, I got confused when I would notice myself procrastinating. What inspired me last week might not be what I'm inspired by today. That big project I started last week no longer feels shiny and bright and I want to move onto the next thing. I haven't finished it yet! I'm feeling resistance to working on it and I'd rather do something else.

I would ask myself, "does this mean that since I'm no longer inspired by this project I should end it and do whatever gives me joy *now*?"

I'm sometimes confused by what feels good at the time and what I should really be doing. There's a lot of things that feel good in the moment and bring me joy, like how watching TV on the couch can be fun. Sure, that seems comfortable and feels good at the time, but there exists an even deeper desire that I'm avoiding.

It comes down to discerning where our desires are coming from. Steve Pavlina says to ask yourself, "where is the path with heart?" You will know the answer.

There are so many distractions all competing for our attention. Every single advertisement is trying to instill a desire in us so we move toward their agenda, not our own. Are we being motivated by our lesser instincts like survival, security, comfort, food, sex, or money? Are we being motivated by social conditioning, peer pressure, or advertising? Or are we being motivated by our higher calling, our heart's desire, or our dreams?

When you are unsure what to do, ask yourself:

Where is the path with the heart? What is my heart's desire? What do I want most?

STEPS TO OVERCOMING PROCRASTINATION

Kill Perfectionism: Lower the bar and make 80 or 90% all you need to do. rule. There's a great video by Seanwes about this.

Break it Down: Tackle big tasks by breaking it down into smaller chunks. Baby steps!

Make it Fun: Focus on the parts you like. Make it fun, add music, listen to an audiobook or podcast, add friends, etc.

Eliminate Distractions: Turn off the Internet, hide your phone, lock the door!

Add Novelty: Shake it up, change locations, try some new clothes or a new app.

Make a List: If we are unclear where to start, make a list. Assess where you are at now and one small step to do next.

Schedule It: If you make it an "event" you are more likely to do it.

PRO TIP: 90-MINUTE FOCUS BLOCKS

One thing I have found that really works is to use two 90-minute focus blocks per work day. Start the work day with a distraction-free focus block right away. This "blocking" of time is also known as the *Pomodoro Technique*. The technique uses a timer to break down work into intervals (traditionally 25 minutes in length), separated by short breaks.

This gives you a regular routine of consistent focus on your most important tasks. If you make this a habit, you will kill procrastination much easier.

For example, after my morning routine, I start work with a 90-minute focus block with no Internet and no distractions. I must do my most important task first. After that, anything goes. I feel accomplished and productive right off the bat. Sure, I don't always do my *best* work every time, but at least I'm showing up!

SHOWING UP IS WHAT COUNTS

So next time you feel distracted or "procrastinatey," check your motivations. You don't always have to choose your higher motivations, but be aware of your choice. Do what you want most, most of the time. If the job seems too hard, lower your expectations a bit or break it into smaller chunks and schedule the time to do it. Get yourself an accountability partner to help keep you inspired. Remember your purpose and reason for doing this because you might have forgotten it.

For more, listen to my podcast on procrastination at http://bit.ly/procrastination-podcast

Overcoming Resistance

Resistance is a close cousin to procrastination. And there's not much I can say about it that hasn't already been covered beautifully by Steven Pressfield in his books *The War of Art*, *Turning Pro*, and *Do the Work*. All short and inspiring reads that cover the dreaded monster that is resistance.

I will do my best to sum up what resistance means to me and how I have experienced it.

Resistance comes up whenever we're motivated by our higher instincts. You know, we want to exercise and get in shape, we want to write a novel, travel the world, spend more time with the family, etc. These are things we put on our bucket lists and make New Year's resolutions for. These are our biggest dreams that we think about all the time as "wouldn't it be nice if." Our motivation for doing them comes from a deeper place within us that strives for something great.

That's all fine and dandy, but when it comes down to doing the work to get there, that's when we face resistance. It's the general feeling of wanting to avoid the task at hand and busying ourselves with something shinier or more appealing in the short term.

I would often get confused when I faced resistance because I thought it might be a message from my higher self alerting me that I shouldn't be doing this. That I'm off my path. And that following my inspiration or curiosity is more important. So I'd stop writing this book and spend an hour online researching some new idea I had. My inspiration and curiosity worked a lot faster than my physical ability to get things done.

I think a lot of people can relate. We start a lot of projects but never finish them. We had a lightning bolt of inspiration one day and if we were lucky enough to even start working on our idea, chances are that we ran out of inspiration and we fizzled out on the project. We shelved it. We either "got busy" or moved onto something new. We probably faced resistance and it felt hard, so we gave up.

But don't worry, this happens to everyone! This is why it's so critical to act on inspiration when it strikes and try to complete the project or task as fast as possible while the inspiration is high. My friend Josh Long wrote a book called *Execute* in only eight days. Guess what it's about? Acting on inspiration as fast as possible.

If you aren't able to complete the task before your inspiration runs dry you'll have to rely on other tactics like breaking it into small chunks or refilling the "inspiration well" throughout the course of the project.

What I was feeling was more likely standard resistance instead of a divine message to give up. Especially if the source of this project came from my own heart's desire. Sure, we face resistance all the time when doing work other people assign us. I think that's different.

When we assign *ourselves* work, like this morning routine for instance, we will face resistance when the inspiration runs out. And then we must shake up our routine by infusing inspiration and curiosity back into it.

From my experience, there are a couple different forms of resistance that I've encountered: external and internal resistance.

EXTERNAL RESISTANCE

This is where other people and situations get in your way to prevent you from doing what you want to do. For example, when you make a move toward a higher goal of yours, people might tell you that you are crazy or try to instill fear and doubt into your mind. Check your motivations and reasons for moving forward. Do you trust yourself? Are you going to let the doubters get to you?

Sometimes when you make change, many people around us will resist. Those close to us like us to stay the same and stay safe, despite what they say otherwise. So be aware of this.

INTERNAL RESISTANCE

This is the nagging voice in our heads that says we aren't good enough. We might have thoughts that try to talk us out of doing what we really want. For example when we are inspired to do something but then our minds rattle off a bunch of reasons not to. Most of those reasons are fear-based and anti-change. Our little minds want us to stay safe and avoid uncertainty, but our higher selves are always pushing for growth and expansion. So it's important to be aware of this voice and recognize it as a sign of internal resistance. Acknowledge those thoughts, but don't let it stop you from taking action on your goal. Maybe the "voice of reason" has some good tips for staying safe while you make a leap of faith. Do so, but don't let those voices stop you dead in your tracks.

Staying Motivated

Staying motivated is a challenge for all of us. Even I, as the author this book, have had many periods where I just didn't care about my morning routine anymore. But eventually I always end up getting back into it someway or another.

I realized it's not the morning routine that matters, but your state of being that matters. In other words, waking up early is a really effective way of reshaping your state of being. And it doesn't end after the routine ends.

The habits you do are also not necessarily the point. I would lose motivation to do my habits. But what I noticed was my state of being. I realized that I would be giving myself grief for waking up late or losing motivation.

I had this fear that if I stopped doing my morning routine, my life would somehow *turn to shit* and I'd be back where I started.

I had put a lot of pressure on my morning routine! Waking up early was only part of it. When I started waking up early, I had a huge reason for it. I wanted to change my life in some way. I needed space and time to myself to focus on building positive habits. And it really did change my life.

But when you wake up at 6 a.m. every day for months, it stops feeling early to you. It becomes the new normal. And then you realize that you are doing the same thing every day and it turns into a rut. It's easy to lose sight of the big picture. You might also not realize how far you've come.

This lack of enthusiasm comes with every habit we try to adapt. Eventually the high wears off and it becomes work. We don't see any immediate changes. We rely on technology to give us virtual high fives as we check in and create streaks of habits. But eventually even that becomes boring.

I end up asking, why am I doing this? Am I getting what I want out of it?

This loss of motivation is different than the lack of motivation we have when trying to start something. This is more like apathy and boredom. There are several reasons why we might lose motivation during our wake up early habit.

REASONS WE LOSE MOTIVATION

- Lost sight of the bigger picture
- Habits become boring
- Seasons change
- Novelty wears off
- No accountability

When we lose site of the bigger picture, we're going through the motions. If you get to the point where your habits become so routine that you don't remember why you're doing it, that's a good step. That means you are doing them automatically. The effects you saw when you started your habit are no longer as evident because you've done it for a while. It might feel more like work.

When you do that, take a step back and reflect. Why are you doing this? What is going on in your life? What are your goals and aspirations? Are you happy? Are you content? What can you change?

Our purpose for waking up early will change and evolve. And it's important to be mindful of this and keep this top of mind.

I do this by regularly doing affirmations, assessments, and reflection. I don't exactly have a big goal I'm shooting for. I enjoy living in the present moment. I can be happy without doing a whole lot these days. But that doesn't mean I should stop creating the life I want. There are things out there I want to do and experience. Am I taking action on those? If not, change your routine to reflect your new goals.

A big reason for lack of motivation is the change of the seasons. When winter comes, it makes it harder to get out of bed. There are things we can do to avoid the hibernation mode, like setting the thermostat to warm up the house before we wake up or having a warm beverage to look forward to.

I allowed myself to sleep in during some winter weeks. It actually helped me get reinvigorated and excited. I used this time to reflect and go experience life without a morning routine once again. It was good to get that contrast and gave me ideas.

Sometimes we just need to read a good book that our curiosity and intuition guide us to. If we're lacking motivation, there are many books out there that will give you a fresh perspective. I loved *The Miracle Morning*, *The Slight Edge*, and the *Power of Now*.

It also helps to get an accountability partner.

Find a friend or someone else who does the wake up early habit with you. Find someone as passionate about personal development as you. Can't find anyone in person, then go online. The *Coach.me* app makes this easy in that you can interact with others also doing the habit. You can ask questions like "how do you stay motivated?" And get some good responses.

You could even hire an accountability coach. I work with lots of clients this way. They will hire me to personally cheer them on, give them personal tips, listen to their struggles, and answer questions. *Coach.me* has this feature built in, but there are many ways you can work with a coach.

When you think about it, every professional athlete has a coach. You don't succeed in the Olympics or in pro sports without a coach. Why should the things we are interested in be any different?

Dealing With Burnout

Burnout and apathy are two major enemies of our morning routines. We start our routines with so much energy and excitement. We dive in head first and we seem unstoppable.

There were periods where I felt like I was on fire. I couldn't wait to get out of bed and I was devouring books and living off the high of inspiration. Everything felt easy.

But then I started to lose the inspiration. I no longer wanted to read anything. I felt lazy and tired. I didn't want to get out of bed. I let simple obstacles completely obliterate my routine. I just didn't care.

I had been doing my routine for about four to five months at this point. I had reached a saturation point and everything started to look bleak.

I had a fear that if I stopped my routine I would slip back into depression or somehow devolve into the person I used to be. It was too cold in the house and I didn't want to get out of bed. I fell back into habits of snoozing and procrastinating. I no longer exercised, took walks, and was slipping up on my meditation habits.

I was burned out. I was apathetic. I would beat myself up about it and feel guilty. But what did I do to get myself out of it? I accepted it.

I let myself hibernate for the winter. The Christmas holiday came and went and the new year arrived. Throughout this time I was filled with family obligations and distractions. I wasn't working during the holiday break so I wanted to sleep in more. This type of forgiveness and flexibility increases the likelihood of long term success.

Around this time I was having more lucid dreams and out-of-body experiences. Naturally this lined up with sleeping more.

While my wake up early habit subsided, I continued to meditate and write in my journal, maybe with less enthusiasm than before. I still read books and listened to podcasts if they really grabbed my interest.

I didn't let it get me down. I knew I would bounce back and eventually start my waking early habit again. It was actually good that this experience happened because it allowed me to contract a little. While I spent several months consuming information and trying new habits, there came a time for putting it aside a little.

Doing so helped put things in perspective for me. It allowed me to look at my life as it was now and how my routine fit into my schedule. Did I even want to do it anymore? I gave myself the option to say "yes" or "no."

GIVE YOURSELF AN OUT

The idea of not having to do my routine anymore was actually a relief. I no longer felt like I had to keep it up just to keep it up. I didn't have to keep some arbitrary streak alive. It helped me learn that there are ebbs and flows. Periods of expansion and contraction, exertion and rest.

I readjusted my routines and added something different for each day. I gave each morning a focus instead of just doing the same old thing. That helped energize me and get me looking forward to it.

The point is, burnout and apathy will happen sooner or later. The harder you go, the faster burnout will happen. But realize this is just temporary and is a great opportunity to reassess your life and your goals. Reflect on how far you have come and spice up your routine with some new goals and habits.

We are constantly evolving as humans. We adapt no matter what gets thrown at us. What starts off exciting will soon become normal. This is why it's important to follow your excitement and not some predictable routine. You will be excited about different things at different times. Pay attention and let that be your guide to where you go next.

But I Have Kids

I've had people tell me that they would love to get up early but they can't because they have kids. I can't truly understand their situation, not having kids of my own, but I do sympathize with them. I do believe that anything we want is possible if we want it badly enough.

Productivity and wellness coach Rob Filardo says, "For me, it is about unexpected situations. It isn't unusual to have our five-year-old sleepwalk into our bedroom at 3 a.m. after I stayed up till 1 a.m. Sometimes my two-year-old will wake up screaming *minutes* after I woke up at 5:30 ready for a great morning routine."

Leo Babauta has several children and he still makes time to get up early before everyone else. I think that is an even bigger motivator to wake up early because otherwise, you are really starved for time to yourself. Carving out time for yourself becomes much more impactful when you don't get much during the day.

169

This applies to living with roommates or a spouse or anyone else for that matter. It's a fact, having other people in the house definitely affects our routines and our autonomy. We have obligations to other people that sometimes make things challenging for us.

Having children or other obligations can also act as a brilliant motivator. If you have other people depending on you for things, you are more likely to stick to your habit. It's a subtle accountability partner.

A friend of mine who recently started a wake up early habit suggested making breakfast for your spouse every morning. I thought that was a great idea because it combines waking early with a light responsibility to someone else. This will hold you accountable to some degree because someone is counting on you. Not to mention you make your spouse happy!

Having children might mean you don't get much sleep at night. Especially if they are young. If you really want to get up early and build an epic morning routine, but are responsible for caring for children at random hours in the night, it will be difficult.

"It is about the intention of getting up early coupled with the flexibility and understanding (which can be strengthened with meditation) to accept that sometimes when unexpected situations change you will have to try again tomorrow," adds coach Rob Filardo.

You have to take a look at your priorities and decide which is more important to you. Maybe there's a way to find a balance. I just don't like to hear people lament about how they wish they could find time to do what they want but they just can't. This would be blaming others and not taking personal responsibility for your desires.

I know that sometimes we get ourselves in situations where our desires are put on hold, but don't let that become your norm.

Having said all that, I think you can find a balance or happy medium. Do something positive that takes one step toward your goals. Maybe that means waking up only one hour earlier a couple days a week. Make sure you communicate to your family or to those that might be affected by your new schedule and resolve any issues that come up. But the truth is, you can do it. There is a way!

Read more: Rob Filardo on how meditation made him a better Dad - http://bit.ly/meditation-dad

Experimenting With Seasons

Seasons are a relatively new concept to me. You know how TV shows and professional sports are organized in seasons? Why don't we apply those same methodologies to our own life and our own projects?

Often when we start something we don't think about how it will end. We want to pursue it forever! When I started waking up early, I didn't exactly know when I'd stop doing it. I had the idea that I would go on doing it as long as I could until it became a habit.

A great example is a podcast. When we started the *Go Media Podcast* in 2012, we put out one episode at a time and eventually we started to lose our enthusiasm. Time between episodes increased and eventually we fizzled out and stopped making new episodes. Other priorities got in the way.

Instead of fizzling out like this, what if there was a set goal of doing a certain amount of shows, just like a TV series?

What if you could do that with your morning routine? Get up two hours early for three months and then take a month off. Then do three more months with a new perspective.

A friend of mine does this with exercise. He has periods of intense training and also periods of no exercise. It helps prevent us from the inevitable burnout and fizzle that so often happens when we commit to something with no end in sight.

Life is kind of like that anyway. If we look back we can identify some definite seasons. Times in our lives that were centered around a location, relationship, a job, a goal, etc. And when those ended, your life didn't end. It just evolved into another season.

I know for me, ending things is always hard. I often feel like it's a "giving up" on a project. If we take the perspective of seasons, we can find relief knowing that things always start and end, start and end, *ad infinitum.*

When starting a project or new habit, decide in advance if you want to do it forever or only for a season. You get to decide. Maybe a season is the right thing to do to take pressure off you for making a long term commitment. After the season is up, you are free to reassess and decide if you want to "renew" for another season. Cool, huh?

ഹൗര

It's Easier With Friends

It's always more fun when other people are on the dance floor. I like to say this because our energy and enthusiasm increases when we see other people doing what we are doing.

When you start a wake up early habit, it can feel pretty lonely. That's kind of the point, it's carving out time for yourself, right?

But when we begin new habits, it can be hard to stick with them. Having friends or accountability partners there to motivate us works wonders.

In *Coach.me*, you are able to connect with other people attempting the same habits you are. You can see other people checking in and asking questions. You can ask questions yourself and get support. We all know the power of the community and how it can help motivate us and get us out of a funk.

I suggest you find yourself an accountability partner. Someone who will do the wake up early habit with you. Get them a copy of this book so they understand how exciting it can be. When the two of you do this together it will increase your chances of sticking to the habit. Not to mention make it more fun.

What I've seen a lot of people doing lately is hiring coaches. I started doing this ever since I took my first drum lesson when I was 25. Not only was I paying to learn how to drum, but I was really paying for the accountability. Someone to motivate and inspire me. Someone to be there for me when I was having trouble.

The same thing happened when I wanted to get back into break dancing. Break dancing is one of those things that's really hard to do on your own. Trust me, I've tried to practice by myself and it was tough to find the energy. When you're around others who are dancing, you feed off each other's energy.

Most recently I've been working with a life coach and we call each other once a week and share our goals and habits. She texts me updates on what she did that day and I regularly update her on the progress of writing this book. I can't tell you how much better this makes me feel about doing what I'm doing. Having someone to bounce ideas off of that supports you 100% is a beautiful thing.

If you're interested in hiring a coach, *Coach.me* features private coaching services on any goal you can imagine. In fact, I was invited to be a coach in the app after they read my post about waking up early for a year. I jumped at the opportunity because I love the idea of other people doing the wake up early habit with me. And to be able to share everything I've learned and help people directly was awesome.

I'm available for hire as a coach through their app and I also do private phone or Skype sessions.

CHAPTER FIVE

ALWAYS BE LEARNING

The thing that really gets me going is constantly learning and experiencing new things. As humans, we are drawn to expand our knowledge and better ourselves. My favorite way to stay inspired is to let my intuition guide me to new learning experiences.

In this section, I'll talk about the importance of reading, listening, watching, and experiencing.

ಬಿಂಬ

Life-Changing Reading Habits

When I was a kid, I hated reading. In 5th grade I got my first F on my report card in reading class. That was the same year I failed to read a single book for the Reading Auction, where the more books you read, the more fake money you earned so you could spend it on more books and other goodies at the big event at the end. I didn't read a single book!

I tried though. I chose Shel Silverstein's poetry books, but I was told those didn't count. Nothing else interested me! I managed to read just enough to get through high school English class and I had to read a few text books for college. Until then, reading was a chore. Reading was an assignment. I saw other kids reading stuff for *fun* and I didn't get it.

There was a time when I tried to read for fun. It was a choose-your-own-adventure book and I remember it being somewhat entertaining. I felt accomplished while reading it.

WAKE UP

At some point things switched. Near the end of college, I read a newspaper review of a book called *The Epidemic*. It was a non-fiction book about the next generation of children growing up with permissive or absentee parents and society's reliance on behavior medication. The book's author was saying it was creating an epidemic of soulless and lifeless children who were more robotic than human. It piqued my interest so I bought it.

That was the first book that I ever bought and finished. I enjoyed it! I read a few other books like *Fast Food Nation*, *Traffic*, and *The Long Tail*. I started noticing that I enjoyed books about society, culture, and why we do the things we do. I noticed that I would actually look forward to reading them. I felt like I was learning something that nobody was teaching me in school.

At that point I became a reader. A person who reads. I also started reading blogs and forums about relationships, psychology, sociology, and eventually, business. I found my niche.

For most of my adult life I was interested in books that bettered me in some way, whether it was reading books about business, marketing, or design. I would shop for books whenever I had a burning desire or question. If I found myself in a rut, I would look for books to get out of the rut. If I found myself looking for marketing ideas, I'd search online for the best reviewed marketing books. I'd end up following my favorite authors and leaders in the design and social media fields.

When I was going through my depression, I bought *Taking the Leap: Freeing Ourselves from Old Habits and Fears* by Pema Chodron. I resonated with the minimalist and loving tone of the book. It was up there with Leo Babauta's *The Power of Less* which was also a game changer for me. I started visualizing a simpler life that was free of clutter and distraction.

At that point I read maybe three to five books per year if you count audiobooks, which I'm a huge fan of. But something changed around that time.

WAKE UP

I started reading book after book. Each one would turn me onto a new idea or author that I would look up and save their books to my wish list.

Sean Webb's *I Am Spirituality* podcast opened my mind to so many more books. This was my introduction to spirituality, the ego, Buddhism, and meditation. He would recommend books all the time and I couldn't seem to keep up! One of the first few books he recommended was *The Power of Now* by Eckhart Tolle. That blew my mind and changed how I saw reality.

This was around the same time that I had my first out-of-body experience. An out-of-body experience is very similar to a lucid dream but with a sensation of floating out of your body. A coworker let me borrow some books by Robert Monroe, who is the one of the pioneers of this field. I tore through his trilogy of books and kept coming back for more.

I realized I was getting obsessed. I had a voracious appetite for reading. I would be reading several books at any given time. I had audiobooks for when I was doing chores, exercising, or driving. And I had a book on the coffee table and in the bathroom. I couldn't get enough! I was reading several books per month.

There were moments I felt like my mind was going to explode. I had to take a break. But after a couple of days of no reading, I just wanted to get back to it. I was learning so much. I had never felt this inspired. So what happened?

There was something that shifted inside me. Something opened up. As long as I was reading the right type of book, I couldn't put it down. This reading habit became a big part of my morning routine and it definitely changed my life. I feel like reading is critical to expanding your mind and helping you find out who you really are.

You see, I started noticing which books really caught my interest. I let my curiosity lead me. I started reading about topics that I normally would have stayed away from including spirituality, sex, and even aliens. What did this say about me? Why was I so interested in this stuff?

For you, my advice is to let go of your judgments and let your curiosity guide you to your next book. There are so many life-changing books out there. There are lists of books that successful people everywhere continuously recommend, so why not start there? Or if you have a peculiar interest, but don't let yourself explore it, now is the time!

Use your imagination. Read ten pages of a good book every day. Here are a few more of my favorites that you might be interested in.

- A *New Earth* by Eckhart Tolle
- *Personal Development for Smart People* by Steve Pavlina
- *The Holographic Universe* by Michael Talbot
- *Manage Your Day to Day* by Jocelyn K. Glei

For a more complete list of my book recommendations, look me up on Good Reads.

Listening to Podcasts

Another great tactic for learning and staying inspired is listening. When I'm not reading a book, I'm usually listening to an audiobook. But I can't write about learning without talking about podcasts. If you aren't familiar with podcasts, it's basically an independently produced radio show on topics that interest you.

A lot of people find podcasts in iTunes, but I prefer to use a dedicated podcasting app. I use *Pocket Casts* but I have also used *Instacast*. You can search for podcasts within the app.

I listen to a range of podcasts centered around spirituality, productivity, business, and general learning. On the spirituality side, I'm a big fan of *Super Woo Radio* by George Kavassilas, because he interviews so many interesting people. The show blows my mind and I love spending time listening to him. On the productivity and business related end, I love *The Fizzle Show*, *SeanWes Podcast*, and others. And I can't leave out the *Glimpse of*

Brilliance podcast (formerly *Gossipist*), *Stuff You Should Know*, and *This American Life*. So whatever your tastes may be, there's usually a podcast about it. Someone out there has been inspired enough to talk about it, interview others, and post it online.

Listening to podcasts has inspired me to create my own. Back in 2012, with the help of Bryan Garvin, we started the *Go Media Podcast* where we talked about design and business.

That led me to create one for myself to talk about the more esoteric topics I love. The *Maker/Mistaker Podcast* is what it's called. I talk to people about building habits and becoming a creator of your own life experience.

The best part about these podcasts is that I can listen while I drive, wash dishes, or exercise. It's not necessarily about constantly learning, but about spending time in that "energy" so to speak. I love to hear people talk about what I'm into. It's like a conversation that I'm a part of.

Aside from audiobooks and podcasts, there are also some amazing lectures, TED talks, and workshops you can find on YouTube that you can play in the background of whatever activity you're doing. If you really liked a book, chances are the author has some speeches or interviews he/she's done on YouTube.

Watching TV, Movies, and Videos

It's kind of odd that I would talk about watching TV or movies in a book like this. But seriously, we all watch stuff practically every day. But what are you watching? We should all be aware of what content we consume. There's so much of it out there. I cut the cord to my cable subscription years ago and haven't looked back.

You have control over what you watch. For me, I want to watch things that expand my mind and inspire my spirit. Watching movies and videos can help reinforce newly learned ideas and introduce new concepts I might not have been aware of. To me, watching is totally a learning activity. But at the same time, I can't deny it's also an entertaining one as well.

I love documentaries. Netflix and YouTube have tons! Sometimes I would use this as an excuse to wake up early. When I started my morning routine habit, I would wake up and watch a new episode of some addictive TV series. It was a good way to get my body out of bed.

Once I was done with the show, I was more likely to stay up and finish doing some of my other "happy habits" like meditating, journaling, etc.

Whatever your taste is, chances are there are great documentaries about it online. There's a website called TopDocumentaryFilms.com that has an amazing collection of streamable documentaries that are hard to find elsewhere.

If you want to change your life, all you have to do is ask. Type in "inspiring speech" on YouTube and you might be able to guess what come up.

For me, I would use YouTube's "watch later" feature because I kept finding things faster than I had time to view them all.

One thing that stood out to me was that individuals would use YouTube to vlog about their own spiritual and personal development journeys. They would offer advice and answer questions. Gigi Young and Charis Melina Brown are two women who have great indie vlog channels that post really thought-provoking content. Marie Forleo is another woman with a great YouTube channel with a ton of amazing advice.

Take any author of a book you loved and look them up on YouTube. They probably have a talk or interview that you could watch. Or maybe there's a book you don't have time to read, but would benefit from a 30-minute lecture the author gave at some conference discussing the key points. Sometimes that's all there is!

Use these different forms of media to increase your knowledge and awareness of your self and the universe. Look up Alan Watts videos on YouTube because there are many inspiring ones. Watch TED talks that pique your curiosity.

STUFF TO WATCH

Check out my my liked videos and my subscribed channels on YouTube for some thought-provoking content. Not everything I watch will appeal to you, so take what resonates with you and leave what doesn't – http://bit.ly/jeff-youtube

Here's a list of 180 documentaries to expand your mind – http://bit.ly/good-documentaries

Growth Through Direct Experience

Lastly, we can't leave out learning through direct experience. This is what transforms head knowledge into internal knowing. Stuff we read in books is only knowledge, but when we actively try something out and see what it's like, only then we can truly know.

I had been a huge fan of music my whole life. And I'd always wanted to play drums. Since I couldn't play, I started learning how to produce beats in *FL Studio* when I was 18. This was great, but I still wanted to learn.

When I was 25, a friend of mine asked me about starting a band together. I told him I wanted to learn how to play drums and this would be a perfect excuse to try. I found a used drum kit on Craigslist and found a local music studio teaching drum lessons. So I signed up.

I figured if I could just take a few months' worth of drum lessons, that would get me started. This was the first musical instrument that I ever tried hard to learn. It was rough at first, but my only goal was to play that fast punk rock beat so my first band could actually jam together.

It only took me a few weeks to build the coordination to keep a steady beat. I was far from good, but I was good enough to start a band!

I could have learned only so much from watching videos and reading books about drumming. But direct experience is obviously key here.

But what this taught me was that I could take classes like this even as an adult. This inspired me to revisit my love for break dancing. A thing that I used to do in college with my friends. I simply looked online for classes and signed up. Yes, I was nervous, but I was curious and wanted to try anyway. I wanted to learn from a real b-boy, not by watching video tutorials online. And I wanted some accountability and some dedicated time to practice.

My first class was...odd to say the least. It was an all-ages class but I happened to be the only student over the age of 10! Despite the awkwardness, I kept at it. During a freestyle dance session, I accidentally kicked a five-year-old boy in the chest. He started crying and I felt horrible. What a way to make an impression! I was going to quit after that class, but the dance studio convinced me to keep coming back.

Now, this was important because it taught me once again that I could teach myself something. I could find an instructor or mentor for just about anything and learn from him/her. At that time in my life, it was drumming and dancing.

But aside from taking a class, what's another way you can get direct experience? One prime example for me was after I had my first out-of-body experience. Since I experienced this first-hand, I had more knowledge and insight than I would have had if I only read about it. There's so much metaphysical information out there that it can make your head explode, but when you can directly experience the metaphysical, it suddenly puts things into perspective for you.

LEARN AND DO

You can read about the benefits of meditation all you want. But until you try it and experiment, you won't really know. You can learn about productivity and the 10 most successful strategies to make a million dollars, but unless you actively do something with that knowledge, it just sits in your head. I've read dozens of books the past couple years, and most of that knowledge kind of fades away or slips into my subconscious. It's only when I apply that knowledge in reality that I can see what I have learned.

CHAPTER SIX

FINAL THOUGHTS

Thank you for taking time to read this book. As you can see, waking up is a lot more than just getting up early. For me, it's been a life-changing experience.

So what have you learned?

You've learned that by starting and committing to a wake-up-early habit, you can change your life.

You've learned that you can create the life you want by trying new habits and quitting ones that don't serve you. You have learned that meditating and journaling can help you discover your own personal truth and purpose in this life. And you've learned how to overcome the challenges we face when we try to wake up early and take action on our genuine desires.

I hope your journey doesn't end at the end of this book. I want to see you succeed! I want to see what happens to you after YOU wake up early for an entire year. Can you do it?

ഔങ

Resources for Personal Growth

RECOMMENDED BOOKS

- *The Miracle Morning* by Hal Elrod
- *The Power of Habit* by Charles Duhigg
- *The Power of Now* by Eckhart Tolle
- *A New Earth* by Eckhart Tolle
- *Mindfulness in Plain English* by Henepola Gunaratana
- *Personal Development for Smart People* by Steve Pavlina
- *The Slight Edge* by Jeff Olson
- *Do the Work* by Steven Pressfield
- *The War of Art* by Steven Pressfield
- *Turning Pro* by Steven Pressfield
- *The 7 Secrets of the Prolific* by Hillary Rettig
- *How Emotions Work* by Sean Webb
- *Manage your Day to Day* by Jocelyn K. Glei
- *The Power of Less* by Leo Babauta
- *The Way of Liberation* by Adyashanti
- *Execute* by Josh Long
- *The Four Agreements* by Don Miguel Ruiz
- *Dream Year* by Ben Arment
- *The 4-Hour Workweek* by Timothy Ferriss

RECOMMENDED APPS

- *Coach.me*
- *A.M. Routine*
- *Seconds Interval Timer*
- *Headspace*
- *Calm.com*
- *Stop, Breathe & Think*
- *Day One*
- *ToDoist*

RECOMMENDED PODCASTS

- *Maker/Mistaker Podcast*
- *iProcrastinate*
- *Super Woo Radio*
- *Stuff You Should Know*
- *Tim Ferriss Show*
- *I AM Spirituality*
- *Glimpse of Brilliance* (formerly Pillowtok)
- *Seanwes Podcast*
- *Nathan Barry Show*
- *Fizzle Show*
- *Steve Pavlina Podcast*

About the Author

Jeff Finley is an artist, designer, writer, musician, and creative entrepreneur. He was a partner at the design firm Go Media from 2006-2014 and founded Weapons of Mass Creation Fest in 2010. Over the past decade he has lived life based around his passion to create and inspire others.

He wrote Thread's Not Dead in 2010 which helped t-shirt designers launch their clothing companies. Jeff got his start by designing album covers, posters, and merchandise for bands and has launched several design-related businesses while working at Go Media.

JEFF FINLEY

Growing up in the DIY punk music scene, Jeff became very attracted to the sense of authenticity behind the music. This passion has bled into all facets of his life including forming several bands and starting his own festival.

In 2013, Jeff admitted he was going through depression. He started waking up early to focus on his own personal development which led to an awakening and a sense of greater purpose. This inspired him to quit his job and begin a path focused on personal growth and fulfillment.

Read his blog at makermistaker.com

60160978R00129

Made in the USA
Charleston, SC
25 August 2016